**20 Philosophies For Improving
The Quality of Customer Care**

Building Blocks
For Improving Customer
Relationships

*Learning The Difference Between The Concept
of Customer Service and The Demonstration
of Caring For The Customer*

Richard Flint, CSP

❝ Richard always has a way of cutting to the core of an issue and that is no different in this thought-provoking book on Customer Service. He uses several stories, events and circumstances to explore issues and solutions that make this thought-provoking book an interesting and valuable read. The truth is always appropriate. **❞**

— David Linger, EVP, Regional Director, RE/MAX North Central, Inc.

❝ "What happened to America's service culture? Who forgot that without delighted customers appreciating the care they receive from the places where they spend their money, those businesses would struggle to survive? How did the high street retailer and every other customer-facing American business leave the door wide open for internet shopping to move in and steal the retail spending they need to survive? The answers are in Richard's excellent new book. In his usual pragmatic style, Richard will tell you what's missing from your retail offer, how your managers may be turning a blind eye to staff who no longer care about your customers and what you need to do to fix it — fast." **❞**

— Geoff Fitchett, Owner/Managing Director, Go Forward (UK) Ltd.

❝ Richard's <u>Building Blocks For Improving Customer Relationships</u> is a must read for those running customer driven organizations. He unabashedly points out how management teams must embrace themselves as leaders and confront behaviors within the organization at every level which degrade quality customer experience. Richard adroitly identifies the missing ingredient as 'Caring' and provides a roadmap for organizations to embrace it and keep it. **❞**

— Peter Gauthier, City Home Buyers, LLC

" An eye-opening 'must read' for anyone - whether you've been a customer, know a customer or had a customer walk through the door of your business. Richard Flint is a master at knowing what customers need and how to care for them so they come back again and again. "

— **Gerry Biordi, Founder, Sarabella Cooks**

" ...Richard Flint knows what he is talking about and the reader benefits from real life advise that is both practical and useful for everyday administration of any business. I would call it a manager's handbook for basic training of employees; training that cannot be repeated too often as you try to make your business the finest it can be. "

— **Wesley A. Lauer, Esq., Akerman Senterfitt**

" Phenomenal! As President/Owner of a company I was astounded the things we overlook in our daily lives. Customer service is something to be practiced at all levels within a company. This book opened my eyes to realizing how important every person is within an organization. It goes deep into your personal life as well as business. You need to make every person around you feel they are important and make a difference in whatever job or position they hold. Customer Service is for a lifetime ! I can only say this book will be a required reading for all my employees, because it will make a difference for our company, their lives, and many others. "

— **John Louis Hausam, President, ERA John Hausam Realtors**

" Building Blocks for Improving Customer Relationships provides a sure-footed guide to those desiring to better themselves in the world of customer service. "

— **Donna Marie Serritella, President and Founder, Direct Selling Solutions**

Published 2011
Copyright 2011

ISBN# 0-937851-31-0
Flint, Inc. Product #3015

Printed in the United States of America.
For information write to
Richard Flint International
11835 Canon Blvd., Suite C-105
Newport News, VA 23606-2570
or call 1-800-368-8255

info@richardflint.com

www.RichardFlint.com

Cover Design by Denise Smith

DEDICATION

To Fred King whose unwillingness to compromise in customer care built a sales organization with Blue Cross and Blue Shield of Alabama that was second to none. I miss him, but his commitment to taking care of the customer has influenced much of my thinking.

TABLE OF CONTENTS

BUILDING BLOCKS
FOR IMPROVING CUSTOMER RELATIONSHIPS

Building Block #1:
It is not that people in service positions don't understand customer care; the truth is many don't care about the customer.

Building Block #2:
All service oriented companies have a service concept; truth is most do not enforce it and then react when the customer complains.

Building Block #3:
It is not the customer's responsibility to be loyal; it is the company's responsibility to earn their loyalty.

Building Block #4:
Most customers don't expect you to exceed their expectations; they would be happy if you just met them.

Building Block #5:
Most companies only pay attention to the customer when they need them.

Building Block #6:
There is nothing more positive than a person in love with what they are doing with their life.

Building Block #7:
When the customer becomes the enemy, you lose!

Building Block #8:
There is presence whether you are present or not.

Building Block #9:
Customer care is a behavior, not a concept.

Building Block #10:
Be careful what you say; the customer is listening.

Building Block #11:
The number one thing a human wants to know is they matter.

Building Block #12
Never make the customer feel like an intrusion.

Building Block #13
Never keep people who don't care about the customer's experience.

Building Block #14:
People either spend or buy; the difference is defined by the quality of the service they receive.

Building Block #15:
When a company can't admit when they have made a mistake, the customer is made to feel like an idiot.

Building Block #16:
Customer care is just another form of romance.

Building Block #17:
When the customer is wrong, they should be told so.

Building Block #18:
If you are not there to help the customer, you shouldn't be allowed to be there.

Building Block #19:
The real mission of a company is not to get customers in the door; it is to bring them back with a smile.

Building Block #20
When people become a tool to be used, everyone loses.

LAYING THE FOUNDATION
FOR THIS BOOK

You would think with all that has been taught about customer service and with the millions of dollars that have been spent on improving customer service, the quality of customer service in our country would have drastically improved. Reality is *there is probably less customer care than before we started all the emphasis on taking care of the customer.*

You don't have to walk into many businesses in the customer service business before you will come face-to-face with an illustration that demonstrates the lack of quality customer care.

What many businesses fail to understand are the stumbling blocks this creates for building customer loyalty. Every time the customer enters the door of a company in the service business, they enter with expectations in place. Those expectations are either strengthened or destroyed by the people they come in contact with.

Today's customer is less patient. They are tired of being emotionally beaten with trying to do business with companies who are in the customer service business.

Today's customer is less loyal. They know they have several options and are not afraid to take their business somewhere else.

Today's customer is more vocal. When they feel they have been treated wrongly, they are not afraid to stand up for their rights.

Today's customer is more skeptical. Most enter expecting to be treated rudely or have the behavior of the

1

customer representative tell them through their behavior that they don't matter.

Put all this together, and you have a war. The war is between the concept of customer care and what the customer experiences when they enter the company environment. The war is between customers, who want to feel they matter, and those the company hire to demonstrate their commitment to letting the customer know they matter.

Why? Why does this war exist? I believe this war is the result of several trends that have developed in our ego driven, greed directed world of business.

First, *too many talk about taking care of the customer, but their only concern is the bottom line.* When the bottom line is more important than the customer, the customer gets punished. You can talk all you want about how important the customer is, but when decisions are made only to increase profits, the customer gets punished.

Now, don't get me wrong. I believe in making a profit, but I don't believe in punishing the customer in order to pad the company's bottom line. That goes against the meaning of customer care.

Second, *too many companies treat their people as an evil necessity.* They fail to realize the importance of those who come in contact with the customer.

There are two types of customers. There is the "internal customer." This is the employee. This is the person who shows up each day, stands in front of the external customer and demonstrates, through their behavior, how much the company really cares.

The real challenge is the lack of leadership within the company environment. Most companies don't have leadership.

They have management. Oh, they have people at the top who are called leaders, but they are really the protectors of the checkbook. Many at the top are not people people. They are people who are task driven, not people driven. They don't see their job as one of making people feel special and valuable. They are there to protect the bottom line and the stockholders. They are distant and removed from those who are everyday charged with taking care of the customer. They sit in their distant offices making decisions that affect the lives of their internal customers without really understanding who these people are. Their mission is to please a group of shareholders, whose major concern is the company's bottom line. They have forgotten *that profit is the result of quality people doing a quality job of customer care.*

What happens when you put people in a position of taking care of your most valuable asset, your customers, who don't feel they matter to the company? How do you think they feel about going to work each day? Do you think when they arrive they are there to give their best, or to simply do a job in order to receive a paycheck at the end of the week?

Most companies have spent thousands of dollars on creating a mission statement. It hangs on the company's wall, but those in the management ranks don't bother to see if it is actually being fulfilled. They are too busy protecting their space and fighting the fires that are the result of the lack of customer care. Most of those in the rank and file cannot tell you what it says. In most companies it is a hidden mission. It looks good hanging there; it sounds good when you read it, BUT it has very little effect on the behavior of the people.

Most companies have a service policy. They spend time and money training their employees in the art of taking care of the customer. Yet, they don't take the time to monitor whether the service concept is really being delivered by those who stand between management and the external customer. They don't have time; they are too overwhelmed; they are too busy fighting fires; it is not their job. Most don't like the thought of confronting the behavior of those who aren't living up to the responsibility of customer care. It is easier to turn their head or make excuses for what is not happening.

On and on we could go with the reasons they stay hidden in their own world, rather than standing out front making sure the external customer has such a positive experience that makes them want to come back.

Many companies seem to have forgotten that *service is a concept defined each time the customer walks through the door to do business with them.*

It is the "internal" customer that defines to the "external" customer whether they matter or not. When the "internal" customer is not happy, they demonstrate that fact with their behavior with the "external" customer. When the "external" customer comes in contact with an unhappy or unresponsive "internal" customer, the emotional war is fought.

How much money do companies spend trying to get the "external" customer through the door? What happens to those dollars if the "external" customer enters, but is not happy with their experience?

You know the answer to that question. The "external" customer takes their business elsewhere. They choose not to spend their time and money being disrespected by people who don't care whether they are there or not.

If the "external" customer comes back, they do so with an attitude. They have been here before and didn't enjoy the experience. Their previous experience makes them feel it is going to happen all over again. Even if it doesn't, they won't see it. They are jaded by their previous experience and those emotions keep them from seeing what is actually happening.

So many today have chosen to shop on-line. They have decided *the less contact they have with the enemy the better.* The growth of the Internet has provided them with an alternative where they don't have to face the enemy.

If you really look at the psychology of what the internet is doing, *it is strengthening the disconnect between the company and its "external" customer.* The result is the lessening of customer loyalty and a greater emphasis on price, which still affects the company's bottom line.

It is tragic when you really stop and look at what is happening. Companies are more interested in the bottom line than they are with those who provide them with their bottom line.

Management is too exhausted to hold the internal customer accountable for their behavior. It is easier to hide in their world of reasons and excuses than face the truth that is staring them in the face.

They have put an internal customer who doesn't feel valuable, feels under-appreciated, doesn't want to be there and feels overworked, on the firing line to tell the external customer *they matter.*

Then, there is the external customer who is simply trying to resolve a need and feel good about their experience having to work through those who are at war with them.

The answer to this war is simple. It is companies re-establishing the customer, both internal and external, as their top priority.

It is management evolving to leadership. This means increasing their presence with a consistent persistency of taking care of the customer, be it the internal or external customer. It is redefining the company environment with the internal customer treating the external customer with respect and quality care.

It is the entire company believing and accepting their real mission — *quality people doing a quality job of customer care.*

Say what you want, but it all starts at the top of the company and reaches down to those who have been given the responsibility of creating a healthy environment.

Say what you want, but the truth is the truth. *The behavior of all people in the company environment is consistent with the behavioral design that management has made acceptable.* People are what they are allowed to be. Management may try to make them the reason, but they are actually the result. I am not excusing their behavior, but that behavior is simply what they have been told is acceptable. If their behavior is not acceptable, then management needs to evolve into leadership and hold them accountable. Only when the uncaring internal customers know leadership is serious about the treatment of the external customer will there be a different attitude.

If the external customer is a priority, they must be treated with behaviors that expound the fact *their business is important to the company and that will be demonstrated by the people the company puts in front of them.* If the external customer is REALLY valuable, the internal environment will be designed to demonstrate that fact. Only when customer service is more than a concept will there be a difference.

Until then, the war will be fought between the behavior of the internal customer and the expectations of the external customer.

Building Blocks For Improving Customer Relationships examines twenty principles designed to achieve customer care. Anytime the customer questions their value the company has stumbled. Anytime the customer leaves disappointed, leadership has failed in their mission of customer care. Anytime the customer's experience is anything less than positive, there are serious customer care issues that need to be addressed.

Building Blocks For Improving Customer Relationships is a book designed to challenge a company's customer care design and offer insights into creating an environment where the external customer comes back because of their positive experience with the internal customer.

Remember, *when there is emotional disconnect between leadership and their internal customers and that is demonstrated in how the internal customer treats the external customer, you are involved in a war you cannot win.* The customer holds the most important weapon — their money! They know it and aren't afraid to take their business to a company that says through the behavior of all their people – *you, the customer, are our top priority and we will demonstrate that fact by how we treat you!*

THE NAKED TRUTH
It is not that people in service positions don't understand customer care; the truth is many don't care about the customer.

That statement is a tough one to swallow. It is really challenging to accept there are people who have taken jobs requiring customer care, who really don't care about the customer. Each day they get up and go to a job they don't really like. They show up with an attitude demonstrated by behavior that sends the message of *I am here, but I don't want to be.*

It makes no difference how much training you give them; it doesn't matter how much you talk to them. If they don't want to be there and are not in love with what they are doing, their behavior defines that fact to everyone they meet.

Let me give you my definition of the word "Job!" *It's an environment a person goes to each day where they prostitute their self for a pay check!* It is not their passion or their love; it is simply a JOB!

I wish you could have known Fred King. We met over the phone. My program for the Sales and Marketing International Convention had been taped, and somehow ended up in Fred's possession. The program was <u>Understanding Those You Must Trust To Deliver Customer Care</u>. It explained my three internal groups of people that go to work each day.

First, there are the Sponges. These are the people who are new and don't know enough not to be excited. They have a major love affair with what they are doing, and that is demonstrated by the behavior they bring to work.

You cannot miss them. They are eager. They will ask you every question you have ever been asked, more than once. They want to learn and seek every opportunity

9

Products give people a reason
to come to you; your people
give the reason to come back
or go somewhere else.

to gather knowledge. That is a great attribute unless they are with a manager who is overwhelmed and doesn't have time for their questions. That chases them off and makes them feel that asking questions is wrong.

Remember this fact – *someone in the company environment is going to train them!*

They are also very excited. Their energy level is extremely high. They get to work early, are willing to stay late and will do anything you ask them to do. That excitement is contagious. Others, including management, will feed off it.

They are also naïve. Because they are young, inexperienced and not totally mature, they don't know the difference between fact and fiction. Therefore, they are easy prey for the negative people in the environment. They naively believe that everyone wants them to succeed and are there to help them grow.

These Sponges are team players. They are loyal and support whatever the company wants to do. They are willing to do anything at anytime.

They don't have a history. That means they don't bring a lot of negative baggage with them. Since they don't have a history, you can train them in the correct way.

They are a special part of the company. This is the foundation you have to build your future on. The challenge is keeping them. Too many leave before their presence has really been established. They are chased off by management that doesn't have time for them, or the negative people, who are constantly feeding them a diet of misinformation. When you lose your Sponges, you are losing the strength of your future growth.

The next group is your Spectators. These are the people

who come to work each day not to work, but to watch.

These are nonproductive people. They will do just enough to keep you off their back. Don't ask them to stay late or do anything extra.

These Spectators are non-supportive. Their behavior is designed to oppose whatever management wants them to do that they don't want to do. They have their own agenda and I promise you, most of the time it is not the same agenda as management.

They are great with gossip; they are always late for work; they never put in a full day; they feel they are never paid enough; they are always complaining.

The issue here is how they use their negative behavior. Most of the sharing they do is with the other Spectators or with the little immature Sponges. They really have a mission to bring them into the herd of Spectators or chase them off. They know how vulnerable the Sponges are, and they use that to control them. Remember, *someone is going to train the Sponges!*

These Spectators are not a team player. They keep the environment in turmoil. Their behavior is such that it is always causing confusion, chaos and fires for management to fight.

Why does management keep them? Two major reasons. First, management has bought into the idea *there are not a lot of quality people out there.* They are fearful if they let them go, they will not be able to replace them. On several occasions I have been told, "Having them is better than not having a person to do the job. While they are not my favorite people, they do get some things done."

What a sick reason for keeping someone who doesn't care and is not supportive of the mission to improve the company. The simple truth is there are lots of quality people looking for work, but until management let's go of their excuse for keeping them, they will continue to justify their existence. The second reason management keeps them is many are very good at what they do. Many of these Spectators are very skilled and can deliver a quality product – *when they want to.* So, management tends to judge their value by the end product. They don't want to face the issue of what their behavior is doing to the overall environment. It is much easier to make excuses for them than it is to challenge the negative effect they are having on the workplace.

Spectators are the actual internal enemy of the company who are given free reign to act out their agenda. They punish anyone they come in contact with.

The third group is your Camels. These people are the backbone of the company. These are the people you depend on when you really need to get things done on time and correct.

They are consistent. That takes a lot of stress off management. They don't have to worry about the quality of what they do or how they do it. They trust them.

They are persistent. They don't walk away when things get tough; they don't do a job half-heartedly. If something needs to be done, they will stay and do it and never complain.

These Camels are business partners. They treat the business like it was their own. They understand the importance of reputation and work to protect theirs and the reputation of the company.

They are also totally honest. Don't ask them what they think if you don't want to hear an honest answer. They do not play games. Their commitment to quality demonstrates the company's definition of true customer care.

The challenge with the Camels is *they are the #1 group leaving companies today.* Many are retiring; others are taking early buyouts; others are going to companies where the environment is not controlled by the Spectators.

The Camels have grown tired of being asked to clean up the messes the Spectators have made. They are tired of being asked to do more, while the Spectators are allowed to show up and do less.

Ask any manager who has lost a Camel, and they will tell you, *you don't fill the void their departure creates.* When you lose your strength, you have to become weaker.

Ok, back to Fred. He had listened to the tape so many times he had worn it out. He called the office and wanted to get another copy. He also wanted to talk to our marketing department about bringing me to Birmingham for the local Sales and Marketing Chapter. My visit to Birmingham started a friendship that lasted until his death in 1999. When Fred died, I lost my best friend. We spent many hours sitting on his back porch or playing golf talking about the missing ingredient in most companies — *people who really care about what they are doing and the presence they are given by management that won't confront their behavior.*

As the Regional Manager for Blue Cross and Blue Shield in Alabama, his mission was to create a sales force that was totally customer focused. In his mind his primary customers were his people, the internal customer. Their customers were the new and existing policyholders. When you talked to Fred, you knew how seriously he took the mission of taking care of the internal and external customer. On this matter there was no compromising.

One hot and muggy Saturday in July, we were

attempting to master the Blue Monster Golf Course at the Doral Golf Resort and Spa in Miami. Neither of us was the greatest golfer, but we both enjoyed the game. We were waiting to tee off on the eighth hole when I said to him. "Hey, I have a question I want to ask you. Your folks have just won the top service award from Blue Cross and Blue Shield. That is a great honor. What would you say has allowed you to create such a group of business partners?"

He stared into the distance and knowing Fred, I knew he was putting his thoughts together. I learned that Fred never spoke until he had a picture of what he was going to say. "I think the one thing that turned me around and in turn, turned my people around, was me overcoming my fear of losing people. I used to think I could save everyone. I would put my heart and soul into people who didn't want to be saved. They were who they were and didn't want to be any better. I would make excuses for them and tell myself things would improve. Over the years I learned I couldn't make people into what they didn't want to become. So, that left me with a choice. Keep them and change my mission, or let them go and stay true to my principles. I chose staying true to my principles. It didn't take long for everyone to realize I was serious about customer care. They figured out I wasn't afraid to let them go. Once they understood that, the entire culture improved."

There was this long pause and the little grin Fred got on his face when he was about to share a point of wisdom. "Know what I find strange?"

"Tell me."

"These people I let go just didn't care. It wasn't the fact they didn't understand the mission; they simply didn't care. To keep them would have been to lie to myself and the

15

others I had shared the mission with. That would have cost me their respect. Leaders don't fear losing those who don't care. Managers simply make excuses for them and let them have their way."

Fred was so right. It is not that people in service positions don't understand the mission of customer care; the truth is many just don't care. That means no matter what the company feels about the importance of the customer, they are going to live with their own agenda. This is a real test for those who have been given the responsibility of leadership. They can either step up as leaders and challenge the behavior or be a manager that avoids the non-caring behavior of the Spectators and give them control. When the uncaring are given control, those who really care will soon go away. The result is an environment that is not customer friendly and at war with those who keep them in business. The solution is not difficult to understand. The challenge is creating leaders who hold people accountable to the mission of customer care.

Customer Care Questions:
- *Do you work with any Spectators?*
- *Is your boss a leader or manager?*
- *Does your company practice customer care or simply talk about it?*

Real Customer Care Involves:
  C   concern for the customer's experience
  A   a leader that really leads
  R   refusing to lower the standards
  E   environment that is customer focused

AND THE MISSION IS

All service oriented companies have a service concept; truth is most do not enforce it and then react when the customer complains.

Century 21 Traditional was a very good company. The leader was Daisy Burlingame. Daisy was a person who understood the value of the customer's experience to growing a business. I met Daisy at a Century 21 International Convention where I was speaking. During my session, I mentioned, "Each year I take on five companies that I work with. My mission is to help them improve the quality of who they are and create a presence that has a presence when they aren't present."

I believe competition is created because the public looks at two companies that are in the same industry and cannot see any difference. When there is no visual difference to the customer, there is competition for their business. When one stands taller in the eyes of the customer, there is not competition. Competition is really the result of sameness, not improvement.

Daisy asked, "Would you be willing to look at my company and see if you would work with us? I am so committed to improving our understanding of quality customer care."

I was going to be in Southern California and told Daisy I would take a look at the company. The day I was there was the Beginning of The Year Kick Off Rally.

No one really knew who I was. With over 300 agents, most figured I was just one of the new ones. I sat in the back of the room and listened as Daisy and her Sales Manager talked about their mission of customer focus. It was clear this was

Any mission statement
is only valuable if it is
implemented and supported
by all the people.

more than an emphasis; it was a mission. Daisy presented a mission focus that challenged each person in the company to make the customer a higher priority in their life.

"After all," she said, "The customer is what keeps us in business. If we are to be better, we must improve our presence with our customers."

At the conclusion, Daisy asked her people, "Are you with me in this mission of improving our customer care?"

There was a thunderous applause. The meeting ended, and I walked out behind two men who were in management. They were shaking their head in disbelief. One turned to the other and said, "that was a bunch of crap. Our agents don't care about the customers; they only care about the commissions."

The other shook his head in agreement and responded. "It is just going to mean more work for us. She is going to expect us to make this happen. That will simply be a waste of time."

I made note of the names of the two guys and later when my journey with the company began, they were the first ones I wanted to talk to.

I asked them to join Daisy, Paul and me for lunch. "You don't remember me, but I was present at the Kickoff Meeting and walked out behind the two of you. The comments you both made told me you weren't with the program of improving customer care. In fact, you both saw it as a joke. I need to know where you are with the company's mission of improving the quality of customer care?"

I wish you could have seen the look on their faces. They turned white, then red and then remained pale. Daisy, Paul, nor myself didn't say a word. We just sat there waiting for them to respond to my question.

They looked at each other and finally one of them said. "We were only kidding that day. We believe in the mission and support it 100%."

The review of their offices said another story. It wasn't long after that luncheon the decision was made to let them go.

What good is it for a company to have a customer care mission if it is not supported by those who have to implement it? It becomes another point of confusion within the company.

I am a firm believer that people have to know the rules, and that the rules are not simply statements. They need to know leadership is together in the commitment to the mission and the mission is the focus of the company.

If a mission is stated and not lived up to, it is simply a lie. If a mission is stated and people not held accountable, then management becomes a joke and the people lose respect for them.

I was interviewing a company in New Mexico and I asked the CEO, "Do you have a mission statement?"

"Yes, we do. We spent months creating it. In fact as you walk through the company, you will see it hanging in several different places."

One of our first stops was in the Company dining area where several of his managers were having coffee and talking. I walked over and said. "May I ask you a question?"

They looked up at me and the CEO standing next to me and said. "Sure. Ask us anything you want."

"Can you share with me the mission statement of the company?"

There was this look of surprise and fright on their faces. You could tell they were not expecting that question. They muttered and they rambled, but it was apparent none of them could tell me the mission statement the company had spent so much time and money developing.

The CEO didn't say anything, but the look on his face said everything. We walked a little further down the hall and came to their sales training classroom. They happened to have their sales force in for training. There was a group standing in the hall just shooting the breeze. I walked over, paused and said. "Can I ask you a question?"

They paused looked at me, saw that the CEO was standing with me and said, "Sure."

"Can any of you tell me what the mission statement of the company says?"

There was total silence as they each looked at each other. They stammered and stuttered, and finally one gentleman spoke up and told me what it said.

"Thank you very much," I said as we walked away. "Who was that?" I asked the CEO.

"He's our top salesperson in the company. He has received our top sales and customer satisfaction award for the past three years."

I looked at him and he said, "You don't have to say anything. I know what you were showing me. It seems our mission is a hidden mission. I have some work to do with my managers. They should know that mission statement by heart."

He stopped, looked out the window and faced me with this look of disappointment. "How are we going to improve the culture of this company if no one knows the mission we are on? This is really frightening. We spent a year and a lot of money putting this concept together. We involved the management team. Several of those guys you asked were on the committee that put this together. I guess they were doing it for everyone else and not themselves. This is not good."

What a message that sent through the company. I promise you later that week there was a serious managers meeting.

Do you think this is any different from what happens in most companies? I can tell you, it is not. Mission statements are good, but what value do they have if they simply hang on the wall? The mission is a lie if it is not the driving force behind the behavior of the people.

The purpose of a mission statement should be to provide a common behavioral agenda for all the people. It should state the company's commitment to customer care. It should form a foundation of principles that states to the external customer what they can expect and will receive when doing business with the company.

Any mission statement is only valuable if it is implemented and supported by all the people. If management doesn't support it and the people don't deliver the promise, it is simply a concept being used to con the external customer.

If the mission statement is shared with the external customer and not delivered by those within the company they come in contact with, it just adds fuel to the confusion the customer is feeling. It is a simple statement, but one with a lot of truth. *Don't promise if you cannot deliver.* It is better to create no expectations than to create expectations you don't deliver. The external customer will always remember their disappointments.

Customer Care Questions:
- *Does your company have a mission statement and if so, do you know what it says?*
- *Do you think a mission statement is important?*
- *What would your mission statement say?*

Why Is A Mission Statement Important?
M   making of a common agenda
I   investment in creating a partnership
S   states your purpose
S   states what customers can expect
I   influence peoples' behavior
O   organizational foundation
N   no solid direction without it

CUSTOMER LOYALTY
It is not the customer's responsibility to be loyal; it is the company's responsibility to earn their loyalty.

I cannot begin to tell you how many times I have heard a salesperson say, "Customers aren't loyal!" Each time I hear that statement my response is the same. *What have you done to earn their loyalty?*

I am not sure where the idea of customer loyalty came from, but whoever invented it missed the real message that needs to be sent. It really is not the customer's responsibility to be loyal to a company. Customer loyalty is something that has to be earned. If the behavior doesn't earn the customer's loyalty, it shouldn't be given.

Several years ago I owned a home in a subdivision in West Palm Beach called Saratoga Bay. When Karen and I decided to get married and live in Virginia, we made the decision to sell it. I did my research and found a Realtor team of two young ladies who were experts in this area of the Palm Beaches.

When the word got out I was selling, I had lots of Realtors wanting my listing. There was one company I was sure I didn't want to give it to. I knew their reputation from others who had worked with them. I had also done a program for them and saw how they treated their people and how their people treated their customers.

It is a lesson that every company should learn. *Your people are going to treat your customers in the same manner that management treats them.* If that could be understood, it would bring a lot of light to the lack of customer care in many companies.

It is leadership's responsibility to create an environment that earns the customer's loyalty.

I decided to give the listing to these two young ladies, Pat and Carol. They were such a joy to talk to. They were so professional. They laid out what they were going to do, how they were going to market the house and what could be expected from them.

The listing was signed, and we were on our way. Do you know what happened a week later? The company I didn't want to have the listing bought the company Pat and Carol worked with. I wasn't happy, but as long as they had the listing, I could live with it.

A week after the company was sold Pat and Carol asked if they could meet with me. We met at the house and Pat said, "Richard, we cannot work with these people. They don't share the same standards we share. They don't believe in the same level of customer care we are committed to. We have been told we can no longer do it our way. We have to conform to their way of doing things. That is not us, so we have made the decision to leave. In fact, we have already left."

"Where are you going?"

"We are opening our own office and would love to have your listing."

Karen and I looked at each other and didn't have to say anything. We were both thinking the same thing. "We want you to have the listing. I will call the company tomorrow and cancel the listing."

The next day I contacted the company and spoke to the manager of the Bear Lakes Office. I explained to her why I had listed my house with Pat and Carol and since they had left, I wanted to be released from my listing agreement. She told me she would have to check with the owner and would get back to me.

Three days later I received a phone call from her. "Mr. Flint, I have spoken to the owner and he says you cannot be released from your listing agreement. When we bought their company, we also purchased their listings. We own them and are not willing to release them."

Nothing I could say would change their mind. If I owned a company and my customer was not happy, I would give them the right to do business with whomever they wanted to. Not this company. I was told in no uncertain terms "you have three months left on your listing agreement and we will manage and sell your listing."

Realizing they were not going to work with me, I told the manager "If I have to work with you, then this is the person I want to handle my listing."

I told her the agent to which she replied, "I'm sorry, but we have chosen Mark to handle your listing. He is a new agent, but is very good. I'm sure you will be pleased."

I didn't know Mark; I didn't want to know Mark and I guess Mark didn't want to know me. I tried on several occasions to contact him. Each time he was either on the phone or out of the office. During the next three months, our house was shown three times and only four times did Mark have any contact with us.

It made no difference how many times I called and talked to the manager. Each time I would get the same story. "I'm sorry Mark hasn't gotten back to you. I will talk to him and have him call you right away."

Three months went by and we still had the house that should have sold at least two months prior. The listing was up and finally Mark called.

"Mr. Flint, I am so sorry I have been so difficult to

reach. I have a full time job, and it has required more of my time than I expected. Listen, your listing expires in two days and I would like to have it back. I promise I will do a better job. Could I come by tonight and have you sign the papers?"

"Mark, you cannot have the listing again. Your behavior has been very unacceptable; the behavior of your company has been unacceptable. No one told us you were a part time agent. I am not happy with what has been done."

There was this long pause and then these words from Mark. "Whatever happened to customer loyalty? If you will just be patient with me, I will sell your house."

If you know me, you know I am a pretty calm person. This was one time when I was pushed over the edge.

"Mark, you want to talk about customer loyalty. What about your service commitment to us? I have called you twenty four times without you returning one of my calls. You want to talk about customer loyalty. What have you done to deserve us being loyal to you? Tell me one thing; just one thing?"

There was nothing but silence on the other end of the phone. Finally, he said, "I'm sorry." That was the end of the conversation.

The next morning I received a call from Mark's manager. She wanted to explain Mark's behavior during the listing time.

"Mrs. North," I said, "There is no explaining his behavior. He had a service role to do and he just didn't do it. Why would I want to continue a relationship based on disappointment and frustration?"

"Well, as a company we have been very loyal to you."

"Excuse me," I said, "Loyal to me. Mark does not understand the meaning of loyalty. He doesn't understand the meaning of customer care. He doesn't understand the concept of taking care of the customer. There is no reason for us to even be having this conversation. There has been no loyalty or quality performance here. By the way, the behavior of your agents is a reflection on your leadership skill. I have taught for years that the behavior of any person within a company is the definition of the skills and commitment of the leader. I don't respect Mark and I don't respect you. Now, do you have any further questions?"

The next day I listed the house with Pat and Carol and it was sold in three weeks. Now, you may be thinking, *"Why didn't Pat and Carol sell the house while the other company had it listed?"*

First, the other company made it challenging to do business with them. They wanted their people to sell their listings.

Second, Pat and Carol didn't want to deal with the hassles or the unethical practices of this company. Know what? I can't blame them.

Loyalty is an attribute you earn, not one you get simply because the customer has chosen to do business with you. Loyalty is an attribute that is generated by quality behavior on the part of the company representative.

It is not the customer's responsibility to be loyal to the company. It is the company's responsibility to create an environment that earns the customer's loyalty. If a company or a salesperson wants to know the quality of their customer concern and care, all they need to do is look at the repeat and referral business they get from their customers.

It is not that customers don't want to be loyal. Most would love to develop a relationship with a company where they don't have to worry how they will be treated. Most customers would love to be a loyal customer. The challenge is the fact too many companies are not customer focused enough to earn the customer's loyalty. Then, they get upset when customers are going to the competition.

Rather than seeing this as a sign of a lack of customer care, they turn the spotlight around and make the customer the enemy. They are not the enemy; they are the casualty. When you go to war with the customer, you will not win. They hold the ultimate weapon — *their dollars.*

Customer Care Questions:
- *Do you agree loyalty is something a company must earn?*
- *Do you have companies you no longer shop with because of their lack of customer care?*
- *Is your company good at earning customer loyalty?*

How To Guarantee You Earn The Customer's Loyalty?

E   emotionally stay calm, no matter what
A   always make the customer the top priority
R   reassure the customer at every opportunity
N   never make promises you can't keep

THE DOOR OF DEMONSTRATION
Most customers don't expect you to exceed their expectations;
they would be happy if you just met them.

Every customer has expectations! That is something all companies need to understand. All customers enter the business environment with expectations. The real tragedy is *most people expect to be lied to and disappointed through their experience.*

The track record of most company's experiences with their customers is not healthy. Too many spend their days cleaning up the customer messes that have resulted from the lack of a quality presence.

I recently spent a day with a company to see if I would consider working with them. I sat with their management group talking about customer satisfaction.

The President of the company made a very interesting comment. "Richard, last year I wanted to raise our prices, but couldn't because of all the customer disappointment we had created."

"Are your prices below the industry standard?"

"Yes, our prices are at least 10% below where they should be. We need to raise them, but how do you go to your customers and tell them you are going to raise prices when for the last year, you have been disappointing them with your lack of quality? It doesn't make sense."

I looked at him and said. "The lack of quality is normally the result of one of two things. First, the lack of knowledge and know how in producing a quality product. Second, the lack of employees who really care about the customer. They do perform a task and that's it. Which one do you think fits here?"

33

Don't blame the customer
for wanting value.

There was silence among the entire group of managers. They sat there looking at each other. I knew they knew the answer, but no one wanted to be the first to say it.

Finally, the plant manager looked around the group and said. "If no one wants to say it, I will. Our issue is the lack of people caring about what they are doing."

Another one jumped in and said. "That's the real issue. We have made this product for years. It is not that they don't know how to make it. Many just don't care anymore."

Now that the real issue was on the table the entire group felt safe to talk about it. Another one jumped into the conversation. "You know they don't care because of what they do. They know exactly what the end product needs to look like. Yet, there will be pieces in the wrong place. They have made this product hundreds of times. The reality is they just don't care."

What they were talking about was not a pretty picture, BUT it is a fact; a truth many companies don't want to face. If they faced it, they would be forced to take responsibility for what is happening and then, do something about it.

It seems many believe it is easier to beg for the customer's forgiveness, than face the issues within their own ranks and make the corrections.

It is as if they expect their people to mess up. They enter the business relationship with the customer expecting to have to beg forgiveness and offer a discount to make up for the mistake. What they fail to understand is "I'm sorry" means nothing to a disappointed customer, especially, if the customer has heard it before.

It seems many would rather turn the light away from their real issue, which is *a lack of quality people committed to doing a quality job.*

I see a couple of major issues here. You may not agree with them, and that's okay.

First, is the lack of managers (not leaders) who really care. They know what is happening; they know their people are not measuring up, but it is easier to sit in their management meetings and complain. They won't confront what is happening. I wish they would understand *the behavior of all people is consistent with the design management has established.*

The behavior of people is a leadership issue. Their behavior is because management allows them to be that way. There are rules, but people are not held to them. There are quality procedures, but they are not enforced. It is easier to blame than take responsibility for what their lack of leadership has created. These people are not leaders; they are at the heart of the deterioration of quality.

They must mature to understand the truth to *anything you don't confront, you validate!*

The other issue is a union structure that protects those who don't care. When unions were created, they were very necessary. They did wonders for workers' rights. They stepped in and challenged the behavior of management, and the result was improvement.

Today they seem to be driven by greed. They expect more and more for doing less and less. They have done so much damage to the American work ethic. There is something wrong when a person is paid top wages for producing an inferior product and is not held accountable for their lack of work ethic.

Rather than face themselves, they place the spotlight

on companies that are taking their business out of the country. You cannot blame these companies. The union structure has forced them into a nonprofit position. It is either move or die. If the union really cared about their people, they would face their behavior and address the lack of work ethic within their ranks. They would join forces with the company and together work to strengthen the commitment to quality. If they really cared, they would police their own, rather than making excuses for them. They would be in the forefront in demanding their members have a high standard of work ethic. They would not tolerate those whose only mission is to get more for doing less. They would be the leaders, rather than the excusers.

When those who produce the product don't care about the quality of what they are doing, the external customer gets punished. When the external customer keeps feeling ripped off, they soon don't believe in the company or the product. What are they left to do? They either continue to spend money for a product that is not quality, or they take their greatest weapon and spend it somewhere else.

You can say what you want about foreign products, but the quality of many foreign products surpasses that of its American equal. Don't blame the customer for wanting value. They have the right to expect a quality product. Don't blame the customer for going where they feel they can get value; face the issue that is causing them to go there.

If the quality and value is there, the customer will spend the money. If the quality and value is not there, they will search until they find it. All customers have expectations. That is their right. Meet their expectations, and you have a customer. Exceed their expectations, and you have their loyalty. Disappoint them and you have an enemy who has the most important of all weapons—dollars.

What has happened is disappointment has become greater than satisfaction; company and worker greed is more important than producing value; lowering the standard of quality has become easier than facing the issues of the lack of quality; work ethic has been replaced by worker demands. The result is the loss of belief by the buying public in the products many companies produce.

Customer Care Questions:
- *Do you think the commitment to quality in this country has decreased?*
- *Do you think the customer has the right to take their money where they feel they can get quality?*
- *Should the customer expect quality for the dollars they spend?*

Learning To Repair Trust With The Customer?
T   truth about what you will do
R   refuses to accept anything less than quality
U   understand their disappointments
S   stay focused on them
T   takes notice of their expectations

HOW SOON WE FORGET!
*Most companies only pay attention to the customer
when they need them.*

How important is the customer? Does the customer
really matter? Ask any company, and they will tell you a
resounding "YES!" They will tell you "the customer is the
most important thing in the world." Yet, look at how many
companies treat the customer like the enemy.

If the customer has a question, it is seen as a complaint.
If the customer has expectations, they are a problem. If the
customer asks questions, they are difficult.

When we moved our corporate headquarters from
West Palm Beach to Newport News, Virginia, we needed
an accounting firm. Karen did her research and found an
accounting firm for us to interview. During our meeting with
the partners, we explained our needs and our expectations.
Karen had written all these out and a copy was given to them.

Karen told them, "We are looking for a firm to work
with us. We are used to working with people who become our
business partners."

The meeting ended with everyone in agreement and a
business relationship in place. This was a new firm, and we
felt their hunger would give them an incentive to work closely
with us.

Our relationship with the CPA firm had been in place
for three months when Karen sat down with me to talk about
what was happening with the firm. "Richard," she said with
her stern business look in place. "I am getting the run around
from the accounting firm. When we first met with them, we
shared our expectations. I got the reports I needed at the first

39

Customer care should not
be an effort; it should be
the driving force.

of the month, but since then, they haven't provided me with the financial information we agreed to. I have tried calling, but they don't return my phone calls. If they are returned, it is after we are closed. We need to schedule a meeting and talk with them."

Since I was in town that week, we scheduled a meeting with the same people we had met with before. Being the organized person she is, Karen walked in with her list of expectations everyone had agreed to in hand.

When we arrived, the partners were already gathered in the conference room. The look on their faces told us something was up. "Please sit down," the senior partner said as he motioned us to two appointed chairs. "We have had a meeting about your company and have decided we can no longer handle your business."

I wish you could have seen the look on Karen's face. It was beyond a look of surprise. Gathering her composure, she asked, "Can you tell me why you have come to this decision?"

There was silence as the partners looked at each other and finally the senior partner leaned forward and said, "Your expectations are too high. We feel you demand too much."

"Excuse me! When we met with you in the beginning, I shared with you our expectations," Karen said in a firm, but controlled posture.

"In fact, we sat here in this very room and went through the expectations one-by-one. You told us you could handle this. Now, we are too demanding. How can that be?"

"When we took you on as a client, you were one of our first. At that time we weren't as busy as we are now. With all our other clients we cannot devote the time your company requires. We just think it would be better if you found another accounting firm."

Knowing Karen, I decided to jump into this conversation. "Know what? I think you are correct. It is apparent you don't want our business, and we choose not to do business with anyone who doesn't want to be our business partner. Please have all our records delivered to our office."

I'll never forget Karen's words as we drove back to the office. "We were good enough to help them get started. Now, we are too demanding? They just don't want to do the work they promised."

Isn't it amazing how valuable the customer is when they are needed? At that point they are treated with respect and customer care is a priority, BUT let business grow and the bottom line becomes the only focus and watch customer care go down. It is as if customer care is only an issue when business is not going well. Let business happen and watch how taking care of the customer slips into the shadow.

No greater illustration will ever be found than in the weeks following September 11, 2001. None of us will ever forget where we were on that day. I was in Pigeon Forge, TN doing a program when the Trade Towers were hit. At first you thought *this couldn't be happening.* Then, you realized it was true and the awful deed had been done.

On Thursday of that week I was to be in Atlantic City, on Saturday in Chicago, on Monday in Cleveland and on Wednesday in Lansing. The program on the following day was cancelled, but the rest of the schedule was still in place. I called Delta Airlines and was told that they could not guarantee they could get me to any of these cities. I was one of the lucky ones who had a rental car.

I called Hertz and explained my need. They told me to keep the car as long as I needed it and just let them know where I was going to drop it off. Thanks to them, I was able to drive between Pigeon Forge and Chicago, between Chicago and Cleveland and between Cleveland and Lansing.

The Tuesday of the following week was my first time back on an airplane. Yes, I was nervous, but I was determined I was not going to let a group of people control my life with their acts of terrorism. If I did, they would win, and I wasn't going to run away and hide.

My flight from Lansing to Cincinnati was on a Delta CRJ. This is a small plane that holds about 70 passengers. There were three of us on that flight. As we landed and were taxing to the gate, the flight attendant came to each of us, shook our hands and thanked us for flying with them.

My next flight was from Cincinnati to Orlando on a Delta 767. This is a jumbo jet that holds close to 300 people. There were eleven of us on that plane. As we landed in Orlando and was taxing to the gate, the flight attendants made it a point to come to each of us, shake our hands and thank us for flying.

During this period, the airlines were hurting and struggling to get passengers back. For me it was great. The planes left early, arrived early and your luggage was on the belt when you got to the baggage claim area. The service by the airlines was great. The people at the ticket counters were friendly; the people at the boarding gate were glad to see you and the flight attendants on the plane were actually nice. Several times those of us on the planes commented on, "What a difference this was." I think down deep all of us wondered how long this appreciative attitude would last. We wondered when business came back, would they still be as kind and friendly.

The spirit of *passenger thankfulness* lasted for about

five months. When the average passenger started flying again and the planes were somewhat full, the attitude of the airline service personnel reverted to the pre-September 11th behavior. No longer was there the spirit of *appreciation* from those at the front and boarding counters. No longer was there the handshake and the *thank you* from those on the airplane. It was back to business as usual.

When they were fearful the passenger wasn't coming back, they slowed down and noticed the customer. When their fears were calmed, they got back to treating the passenger as just another person they had to take care of.

Somehow those who work in service industries need to understand the customer is more than just another person to take care of. They are the reason they have a job. Why does it take something as tragic as September 11 to cause companies to realize the importance of the customer? I don't think it is the fear of the customer not coming back as much as it is the fear of them not spending money.

The customer doesn't represent an opportunity to make a statement about the company's commitment to customer care. The customer represents a paycheck. To many in the management/leadership position, the customer isn't an asset; they are the bank that keeps them in business. When companies don't see their customers as valuable, the customer soon reacts with their checkbook, and then, the vicious cycle starts all over again.

Too many times companies don't pay attention to the customer until they are no longer there. Then, they get concerned and increase their efforts to take care of them. Customer care should not be an effort; it should be the mission. Customer care should not be a fearful reaction; it should be an everyday attitude. Customer care should be who you are all the time, not who you become when you are fearful of losing the customer.

Customer Care Questions:
- *Does your company treat the customer with respect all the time?*
- *Do you fear losing your customers?*
- *Do you have a customer friendly attitude?*

What Tells The Customer They Matter?
M   making a fuss over them
A   an attitude of respect
T   talking to, not at them
T   truthfulness
E   emotional connections
R   responding to their needs with a real smile

I Love My Job!
*There is nothing more positive than a person in love
with what they are doing with their life.*

Customer care is about energy. It is about feeling the
excitement of being able to solve the need of the customer.

Customer care is about dedication. It is about making
sure the customer is satisfied with their experience.

Customer care is about presence. It is being there
with the customer while they are standing in your presence. It
means not being too busy to help them; it means making them
your focus, not your nightmare.

Customer care is about spirit. It is about you expressing
your love for what you are doing.

The most important of these is spirit. If you are not in
love with what you have chosen to do with your life, you won't
care about how you do it. If it is just a job, you will treat it as
a job. If what you are doing does not feed your spirit, you will
show up each day dreading what you are about to do. If what
you have chosen to do with your life does not feed your spirit
energy, it will not get your best. You will show up, go through
the routine and express how much you dislike what you are
doing with everyone that you meet. If you are not in love with
what you are doing, you should not be doing it.

How rare do you think it is to find people who are in
love with what they are doing? Do you think 50% of those who
go to work get up everyday excited by what they are about to
do?

How can a person offer quality customer care when
they don't want to be there? How can those who are producing
the products the public will use produce quality when they

When you are not in love with
what you have chosen to do
with your life, your behavior will
demonstrate that fact!

don't want to be there. They are there because it is a job, and
they have to show up to get a check. These people are not
honest. They are lying to themselves and to those they share
time and space with. These people will never understand
quality. Their lack of commitment will cause them to be and
remain average in all they do. They will never find happiness.
They will remain part of the multitude that exist in a job and
don't enjoy what they are doing.

How rare do you think it is to find people who are in
love with what they are doing with their life? I listen to people
everyday talk about how much they hate what they are doing.
I watch people everyday demonstrate through behavior the
fact they are not having fun. I watch people treat others with
disrespect because they are unhappy and all they have to offer
is their unhappiness.

How rare is it to find someone who is in love with what
they have chosen to do with their life? What happens when
you find one? Will you keep going back to them? Will you
look for them when you walk into their business environment?

When I was in high school, I worked in an IGA
Grocery Store. My favorite person in the store was the produce
manager, Archie.

Archie was one of those rare people who was in love
with what he was doing with his life. He saw himself as more
than the produce manager; he was there to make sure the
customers got the best produce possible. He didn't just put the
produce out; he made sure every customer could not pick up a
piece of produce that was not quality. I would watch him trim
lettuce. He didn't just pull the outer leaves off; he shaped that
lettuce into a work of art.

I would ask him, "Archie, why do you take so much time with the produce?"

He would look at me over the tops of those black-rimmed glasses and say, "This is more than just produce. This is the reputation of the store. If people go home and aren't happy, they don't come back. We are not the only store in town, so we have to be better than the others."

He would pause, hold up whatever he was working on and say, "You cannot see what is in a can, but you can see the produce. These people trust that I won't give them anything but the best produce possible. I am not going to let them down."

Archie was 64 when I first met him. Little did he know the impact he had on my life. I remember one day asking him, "When are you going to retire?"

There was that over the glasses look and a stern reply. "I will retire when I die, and then I hope God let's me take care of the produce in heaven."

We laughed and I continued my probing. "Archie, why do you do this? You don't have to work."

He laid down his produce knife, sat down in his chair and handed me a very valuable lesson about life. "Richard, I do this because I love it. I have been the produce manager here for 15 years. Oh, there are days I think I have had enough, but then I go home and think about what else could I do that I would love as much as this. I cannot come up with anything else, so I come back and have another day as produce manager."

He paused and I knew he was about to give me one of his points of wisdom. "Listen to me kid. It is not about what you choose to do with your life. It is about loving what you choose to do with your life. If you don't love what you are doing, don't do it. You will only make yourself and the others around your life miserable."

Can you imagine anyone that committed to produce? He was totally in love with what he had chosen to do with his life. Interesting! The customers knew how committed he was. They would come to him with questions, not just about produce. Archie spent hours out on the floor talking to everyone. His happy spirit was a magnet to all who came into that store. He was unique; he was in love with what he had chosen to do with his life.

I have never forgotten that, and I have never forgotten Archie. His love for what he had chosen to do was a positive lesson I learned and will never forget.

How rare is it to find someone who is in love with what they have chosen to do with their life?

If you are ever in the Palm Beaches and need a manicure or a pedicure you must go to Paris Nails in Wellington. The owners are May and Tony. This young couple is a great example of two people who are in love with each other, with family, with life and with their business. I met May about three years ago while she was working for another nail salon.

I have this "thing" about my hands. When I am on stage in front of people, I think people notice four things about me – my shirt (which I am known for), my hair, my shoes and my hands. Each of these make a statement about how I feel about myself and the people I stand in front of.

I had been going to a nail salon and the young lady who had done my nails for years passed away. I tried several salons, but each time I wasn't satisfied with their business environment. It wasn't they weren't good, but the salon environment was cold. It was the typical attitude of "I am here, but I really don't want to be here." I have a feeling you understand what I am talking about.

I was talking to Claudia, the young lady who does my hair, and was explaining to her the challenge I was having. She stopped in the middle of my haircut, walked around in front of the chair, smiled and said, "You need to go next door and meet May. She is what you are looking for. I promise you she is the person!"

I said, "Ok," finished my haircut, walked out and walked into the nail salon next door and asked to speak to May. The receptionist said, "One minute please," turned and spoke to this young lady at the first nail station. She got up, came over and the look in her eyes spoke volumes. It was one of passion, fun and energy. I thought to myself, "Claudia was right. This is what I am looking for."

That was almost two years ago. During this time, several things have happened that continue to tell me how much she cares about what she is doing. For several years before she and Tony moved to the Palm Beaches, they had their own nail salon in Cleveland. When they came to the Palm Beaches, they worked in different salons. While May would be doing my nails, we would talk about how much fun that had been and how they wanted to get back to doing that. I remember the morning I got a call from May informing me that she was leaving the salon where she was working, and she and Tony had purchased a salon where they would once again be working together. Even though she was telling me this over the phone, I could feel her enthusiasm through the phone line. I was as excited as she was for the two of them.

52

When you walk into their business, Paris Nails, you can feel the energy, the excitement, the passion, not only from May and Tony, but from everyone who works there. There is positive energy; there is a spirit from all who are there that sends the message loud and clear, "We are here because we want to be, not because we just need a job." That spirit is the result of the spirit of May and Tony. This is not a job to them; it is a calling. That may sound strange, but when you talk to them, you feel that.

Recently, May and I were talking about her need to hire two or three nail techs. I will never forget her words. "Richard, I interview people, but I don't feel this is what they really want to do. They want a job. I don't need someone who simply wants a job. I want people who love being a nail tech. I want people here who want to help us continually improve what we are doing. I would rather have an empty station, than bring someone in who is going to be a negative force."

I looked at her and said, "You really love this don't you?"

Those dark eyes sparkled as she looked at me. I really didn't need to hear her answer. Her eyes and smile said everything, but she said in the typical May fashion, "I really love doing this. This is what I want to do with my life. I love what I do!"

That's the key to quality customer care. I have sat in their salon and watched the customer interaction, the customer connection, the customer being cared for. I have listened to the customers talk as they leave, and you just know what May and Tony are doing is strengthening their relationship with their customers. They are building an environment where they will have customers for life. People love doing business with people who are in love with what they are doing.

Everyday people express through their behavior what they feel about what they are doing with their life. When they aren't happy, you will experience it. When they are in love with what they are doing, they will tell you in every way possible.

I know there are the Archie's, the May's and Tony's out there, but they are the exception, rather than the rule. Just pay attention to the behavior of those you come in contact with and listen to what their behavior tells you.

Customer Care Questions:
- *Are you passionate about what you do?*
- *Do you work because you have to or because you want to?*
- *If you work because you have to, do you really give your best to what you are doing?*

What Defines Passion?

P   peace with what you are doing
A   a sense of fulfillment
S   sense of humor with what is
S   stability
I   investing in your personal development
O   ownership for your behavior
N   new possibilities are sought

SHUT UP!
When the customer becomes the enemy, you lose!

Can you imagine a service environment where there is a war between the company's service provider and the paying customer? Doesn't that sound ridiculous? The company is there with a product to provide a service to the customer. The customer is there with their money to pay for a service from the company. You would think this would be an easy thing to achieve. Each achieves what they are there to achieve, and each walks away feeling good about what has happened. So simple, YET in today's business world, it has become so complex.

The company hires people who really don't care about service. These people are managed by managers who are either tired of fighting fires or too busy trying to protect the bottom line to pay attention to what is happening.

The customer arrives with a desire to fulfill a need through spending money. They walk in and come face to face with a person who has declared war, because they don't want to be there.

I mean doesn't this sound down right stupid? Each, the company and the customer, has a mission. If the company fulfills its mission and the customer leaves happy, the result is the growth of the company business. If the company doesn't fulfill its mission of customer care, it will end up struggling to stay in business.

Companies can say what they want, but they are really not in business to sell products. They are in business to provide an environment where people with a need can fulfill that need and be happy with their experience.

Companies can say what they want, but their products

55

It's a shame to watch a
good company be destroyed
by its people.

are not the most important things they have. Their value is created by the people who interact in any way with the customer and let them feel they matter.

If the people who physically interact with the customer don't do a quality job of customer care, there is a war. Reality is *the company cannot win that war.*

If those who service the customer are in a invisible position and don't do a quality job of customer care, there is a war. Reality is *the company cannot win the war.*

If a company goes to war with the customer, they lose. The customer is more powerful than the company. When customers decide they have had enough, they walk away with the treasure — *their dollars.*

As simple as this is, most companies don't get it. They would rather make the customer the enemy than face the people issues inside their own company walls. For some reason, they feel it is easier to find new customers than it is to confront the behavior of their people.

They need to reexamine their concept of customer care. As long as they have a program of customer service, there is going to be war. Customer service is a concept; it is not a demonstration. It is a program companies teach their people. The challenge becomes management following up to make sure the concept has become an action.

Until companies realize *the public doesn't care about or believe in customer service*, the war is going to continue to be fought. What the customer is looking for is a service environment that demonstrates its commitment to them through the action of customer care.

Customer service and customer care may share the word "Customer," but that does not mean they are the same thing. A concept is something we explain, but doesn't mean it gets implemented. The meaning lies in the demonstration to the customer through behavior that the company's representatives care about their presence and their need. Until that happens, there will be the war.

The greatest illustration I know about the difference between "service" and "care" happened several years ago aboard an Eastern jet.

You remember Eastern Airlines? At one time, they were the premier airline in the sky. Then, they forget about the customer and in return, the customer forgot about them. The result is Eastern became a history lesson, not a present day reality.

I was on a flight from Atlanta to Miami, and it had been one of "those" travel days for me. I expect to have one upside down travel day every quarter. This is a travel day when anything that could get turned upside down does.

On my first flight from Syracuse to Atlanta, the plane had a mechanical problem, and we were two hours late. That meant I missed my connection from Atlanta to Miami. The next two flights were sold out, so I got the late night flight. The passengers were a collection of people who had had a day like mine. You could tell from watching the behavior in the waiting area, they were walking an emotional tight rope.

The crew's day had not been much better. All of their flights had been late, and they had been emotionally pushed by people who were fearful of missing their connections. Many passengers believe the flight attendants have the power to keep a plane from taking off without the passenger on board. They don't want to hear "there is nothing I can do. You will have to check with the customer service representative that will greet this flight."

We boarded this late night flight about an hour after we were scheduled to take off. I took my seat 2B, and just began to watch the emotional collisions that were happening. The gentleman across the aisle from me arrived, stored his bag in the overhead, took his jacket off and attempted to hand it to the flight attendant.

As she was approaching, he said, "Miss, would you hang my jacket for me."

She walked right up to his face, looked him square in the eyes and screamed, "Sit down and shut up before I knock you down!"

I wish you could have seen the look of fright in this man's face. He didn't sit down; he fell into his seat, clutched his jacket and didn't say a word. The flight attendant turned and walked back toward the front of the cabin.

There was a hush in the cabin. Everyone had seen and heard what had just happened. I promise you no one was going to ask her for anything.

The guy next to me leaned over and said in a very low voice. "That is one angry lady. I cannot believe she talked to him that way."

He paused, looked at the gentleman who was clutching his jacket and continued. "I have been one of this airline's top passengers for years. They used to be such a great believer in customer service. Lately, I think they have stopped caring. Her behavior is not the exception today. She is actually the majority. It is a shame to watch what was once such a good company be destroyed by its people."

Within minutes, another flight attendant approached the man. She looked at him sitting there with this weird look on his face clutching his jacket. She smiled and said, "If you are tired of hugging that jacket, I'll hang it up for you."

The look on his face said he wasn't sure what to do. Did he hand it to her or continue to hold it? She reached and he reluctantly handed it to her.

During the flight, I walked to the front galley to ask for a bottle of water. The flight attendant who had screamed at the man was the only one standing there.

"I'll bet you have had a bad day today."

"It hasn't been one of my best. I have just had a lot of angry passengers. I think I am tired."

She looked at the man she had screamed at, then looked down, and then at me with this questioning look on her face. "I was wrong to scream at that man."

She paused and slipped into deep thought for a moment. "I guess I should apologize to him. I was just taking my day out on him. That wasn't right."

"I think he would appreciate an apology from you. He was really confused by your behavior."

Later in the flight, she did apologize to him. He smiled, but the look on his face said the damage had already been done.

She had chosen to go to war with him. She lost and on a larger scale, Eastern Airlines lost big time. Talk to people who used to fly Eastern, and they will tell you "at one time it was the best airline in the sky." But for some reason yet to be explained, the airline went to war. The first war was fought between top management and the unions. Then, the conflict spread from an inside war to an all out war where the paying passenger was placed in the middle and became the emotional shooting gallery. Someone should have told them. *You cannot go to war with your customers and win.*

All companies share two things:
- products
- people

The products get you noticed; the people get you either remembered or forgotten. Too many companies place their emphasis on the product and forget about their people. The good and great companies place their emphasis on the people first and the product second. They understand people create your reputation. Reputation is not something you can buy; it is a result. Reputation is the result of the public coming in contact with all aspects of your company. Reputation is the customers defining who you are, how good you are at taking care of them and whether they want to continue a relationship with you. Their feelings define your growth or demise. If you go to war with the customer, you lose.

Customer Care Questions:
- *Is this war being fought in your company?*
- *Does your company keep people who don't care about the customer?*
- *How important do you think reputation is?*

How To Stop The War?
W   work on a common customer agenda
A   a management that really cares
R   refuse to accept less than quality care

WHOOPS!
There is presence whether you are present or not.

So far during my life, there have been five people whose presence in my life has had a major impact on who I am. Understand what I mean about presence. Presence is *what I feel about you after you have been in my life.*

We don't fully understand the effect most people have had on our life until they are no longer there. Why? Because most people are only moments in our lives. They enter, they pause and they move on. There are very few who enter and remain even though they may not physically be there. I have had four of those.

The first was Troy Howell. His presence gave me the courage to stand in the midst of my mother making me feel unworthy, unloved and of no value. His availability to my life when I didn't know where to turn gave me hope and a sense of self-value.

During those times when I questioned the design of my life, I go back to Troy telling me, "Richard, you don't understand what or why this is happening to you. What you must do is trust there is a purpose and believe you will come out on the other side stronger and prepared to make a difference. Don't get so caught up in what has happened that it takes your energy away from learning how to use this experience to improve your life."

Troy continues to live even though he is physically gone. He created a presence in my life that strengthened my foundation.

Then, there was Spencer Hayes. Spencer Hayes was President of the Southwestern Bible Company. His gentle

You don't get to define how good you are; the customer does that with their presence.

firmness caused me to stop running from the pain of my childhood and find the cause that continued to challenge my life.

Spencer's challenge to me was "You cannot run away from yourself. You have to know that. Look at your life. It hasn't been the best up to this point, but it hasn't been the worst. What do you want to do? Do you want to keep on running in this self-destructive circle or do you want to move forward and find out what you can really do? Those are your choices. I vote we stop running and find out who Richard is and what he can become."

I have never forgotten that conversation with Spencer. He entered my life at a time when I was more confused than I had ever been. I was tired of running in my circle of sameness, but didn't know how to get out. I was tired of pretending and wanted to just be me. I didn't know who that was, but I wanted to find out. His caring presence slowed me down and gave me the calmness I needed to find myself.

Spencer is no longer in my life, but his presence lives forever within me. He has a presence even though he is not present.

The third person was Clyde Irving. Clyde was my sales manager while I was selling Bible books door-to-door for the Southwestern Bible Company. He was one tough person. He refused to attend my personal pity party and wouldn't let me attend either.

I remember this one conversation he had with me. "Richard, you are trying my patience. You have been given a gift few people have. You have been given the gift of communication. You talk and people listen. Your presence commands attention and trust. I don't understand why you chose to throw that away and live crawling around waiting for people to feel sorry for you. Yes, you didn't have the best childhood, but that is yesterday, not today. Today is another beginning. Why don't you let go of all that garbage and get on with living. Don't waste your talent. If you do, God is going to take it away from you. Step up and become the person God has planned for you to be."

His challenge showed me what I was doing. His presence pushed me to stop looking down on myself and backward with my life. His faith in me gave me permission to excel.

Clyde is no longer in my life, but his presence lives forever within me. He has a presence even though he is not present.

The last was my father. From the age of sixteen until I was twenty-six I didn't have a relationship with him. As long as my mother was alive, he was trapped in a circle he didn't know how to get out of.

When my mother died, I had to make a choice. Either I go home for her funeral or go after the funeral and be with my dad. I decided that going to her funeral would be a lie. I made the decision to spend time with my dad after everyone had left him. That time with him began a five year friendship that just got better and better.

At first, we didn't talk much about my childhood. I tried, but you could tell it was just too painful. Over a period of time it became something he wanted to talk about.

"Son," he said the first time he was ready to address the issue. "I am sorry. That was a tough time for me. I didn't agree with your mother, but there was no getting her to change her mind. She didn't like you. She didn't want you around and

I had to make a choice. I didn't agree with the choice, but I did what I had to do. I hope you can forgive me."

I knew that Thursday night when I was sixteen and he brought me my suitcase was tough for him. I knew and never doubted that he loved me.

One other conversation we had showed me his love.

"Did you know I would come by and check on you?"

"Yes. The lady I was living with told me. I was always hoping I would be there when you came by."

"I always made sure you weren't there. I couldn't face you. Did you know I was at your high school graduation?"

"No! You were really there?"

"Yes! I didn't want to miss seeing you graduate from high school. I was in the very back of the balcony. I was really proud of you. I also would check on you with Mr. Luke. He would let me know how you were doing."

"Mr. Luke never let on he was talking to you."

"Son, I cannot begin to tell you how sorry I am about all that happened. I hope you understand that was not what I wanted. I loved you and have always loved you. I don't understand your mother. She was just a very angry person when it came to you."

"I know dad. I have never questioned whether you loved me or not. I don't know what I would have done in your situation. I might have done the same thing. It doesn't matter now. We have our time."

For those last five years of his life, my dad was my best friend. I spent all the time I could with him. We laughed; we fished; we talked. I miss him today. Know what? He is still present in my life. He has a presence even though he is not present.

What does all this have to do with Customer Care?
All companies have a presence. The quality of their presence
determines the loyalty of their customers. If the customer
leaves with a good feeling about their experience, they will
be back. Continuing to do business with a company is the
customer's way of saying "good job."

If the customer leaves with a bad taste about their
experience that means the company has done a bad job of
customer care. Most will not be back. Their disappearance is
their way of saying "you did a bad job."

Presence is all about what the customer remembers
about their experience. If any company wants to know how
good they are, they should monitor their presence with their
customers. I am not talking about mailing out some little
survey on How Well Did We Do. I am talking about calling the
customer and asking them to rate the quality of their customer
care. There are companies that will do the CSI (Customer
Service Index) for you. How can you know where you need
to improve if you are not asking the customer for their input?
How can you strengthen your presence with the customer if
you are not talking to them about their experience? You don't
get to define how good you are; the customer does that with
their presence.

Customer Care Questions:
- *Does your company monitor its presence with its customers?*
- *In the past two years have customer complaints increased?*
- *Could your presence be stronger?*

Strengthening Company Presence Demands:

P   persistent customer monitoring
R   refusing to lower service expectations
E   everyone is continually challenged to step up
N   never underestimate the power of presence
C   clear consistent communication
E   examine by using mystery shoppers

LIAR!
Customer care is a behavior, not a concept.

In most of the previous chapters we have been talking about the need to stop preaching customer service and start delivering customer care. Although many would say these are the same, they are not.

Customer service is actually no more than a concept. It is an idea companies preach to their people. Day in and day out they preach the importance of taking care of the customer. They emphasize the importance of the customer to the company. They highlight the correlation between the customer spending money and the company having money to hire employees.

Many companies have spent thousands upon thousands of dollars on programs to teach the concept of customer service. With all the dollars invested in the concept many have not seen their level of customer service increase.

Personally, I think Corporate America has taken the wrong approach. They are working too hard to change the behavior of people who really don't want to change. They want to show up, do what they have to do and get a paycheck. It seems it would be a better idea to do a better job of interviewing and holding people accountable for their behavior. The challenge is not as much about the people who go to work each day, as it is the lack of management holding them accountable for their behavior.

Many companies have policies and procedures that govern the expectations of people, but lack the management that hold people's feet to the fire. If management doesn't hold people accountable to the policies and procedures they have

The behavior of all people is consistent with the design management has made acceptable.

put in place, then there are no policies and procedures.

Reality is *the behavior of all people is consistent with the design management has made acceptable.* If those who don't care know they can get by with less than customer friendly behavior, they are going to do it.

One manager told me "I don't have time to worry about the behavior of people. I didn't hire on to be a babysitter. I have enough pressure from upper management to make sure we are profitable."

Profit is a result! It is the result of the customer spending money. If the customer doesn't spend money, you can forget about a company being profitable.

The customer spending money is the result of how they are treated by all the people in the company they meet. Those people may be visible or invisible. It doesn't matter. If the customer's experience is not positive, they will take their money and go elsewhere.

When management doesn't care, neither do the people. When management runs from facing the customer care issues, the people who don't care are actually managing the company. When management doesn't like to confront issues, the issues steal the positive energy from the company environment. When the customer comes in contact with this environment, they remember the punishment they have received.

The idea of customer care is really very simple. It is about people taking care of people. It is about making sure the customer has had an experience that makes them want to come back. The real mission of any company should not be to get the customer in the door, but to make sure they want to come back. If you can create that environment, you will never have to worry about the lack of profit.

If you ever get to Mentone, Indiana, go by the local Marathon Station/Convenience Store. Walk in and feel the energy. Those ladies that work there are there to take care of the customer. Their #1 mission is to make sure the customer wants to come back. I was there the day after they opened their new Subway store. You talk about excitement. The energy made you feel good. I told Steve Sands, who was the owner, "This is one good group. They are connected in their energy, understanding in their mission and determined to make everyone smile."

If you ever met Steve Sands, you will not forget him. He is this 6'2" tower of passion. He can't talk about his business, his family or his life without you feeling the passion. That passion rubs off on his people.

In my time with him, I asked him, "What does being in business mean to you?"

He smiled the Sands smile and said, "It is all about people. If you don't have good people inside, you don't get the customers. If you don't get the customers, you don't stay in business. It is all about me as the leader making sure my people know the expectations, have a great environment to work in and enjoy what they are doing."

He is so right! Customer care is simply people taking care of people in a fashion that makes them want to come back. If leadership doesn't state the expectations and hold people to them, there is a lack of customer care.

Several years ago I got stuck one night in Orlando. It was one of those travel days you don't want to have. I was scheduled to arrive in Orlando around six in the evening, but with the weather in Atlanta nothing was on time.

I knew it was going to be late, so I called one of the

hotels close to the airport and booked a room. I had to be in Cocoa Beach the next day, but didn't want to drive late at night.

We arrived in Orlando around one in the morning. I got my luggage, got my rental car and made my way to the hotel. Upon arriving at the front desk, I met Mike. He was not the friendliest person I had ever met. He greeted me with a half hearted, "May I help you?"

"My name is Richard Flint, and I have a reservation."

After I was all checked in, I said, "Mike, I need a wake up call in about three hours. I have to drive to Cocoa Beach for a presentation."

The look on his face said, "That is more information than I care to know."

In three hours my phone rang. As I made my way to the bathroom, I noticed my room bill under my door. It looked thick, so I picked it up to discover it was seven pages. I walked back over to the bed, sat down and started going through these seven pages of phone call charges. This was one of these hotels that charged a buck fifty for any phone call—credit card or 800—it didn't matter. There was a $1.50 connection fee.

I was amazed at all the phone calls on my bill. I had come up stairs, gone to bed and not touched the phone. I got dressed and made my way to the front desk where Mike was still present.

"Mike," I said in a calm voice. "We have an opportunity for you to demonstrate customer care."

The look on his face said he had no idea what I was talking about. I laid the bill on the counter and pointed to the seven pages of phone calls.

"Mike, I am being charged for all these phone calls I didn't make."

He looked at me with this look of disgust and said, "You had to make them."

"Excuse me."

"You had to make them. They're on your bill."

"Mike, I didn't make these calls. I went upstairs three hours ago and went to sleep. I didn't make any phone calls."

The look on his face turned from disgust to anger. "What do you want me to do?"

"It is real simple. Take them off my bill."

He grabbed the bill from me and began working on his computer. About fifteen minutes later, he pushed my bill back across the counter, and now my seven-page bill was ten pages. Underneath each phone call log were the words "disputed charge."

What was he calling me? He was calling me a liar. He looked at me and asked with great arrogance, "Are you happy now?"

"No Mike! I am not happy."

The entire time he was playing with my bill I was reading this sign that was behind him that said *the customer is our greatest treasure; treat them with respect.*

"Mike, do me a favor. Turn around and read that sign behind you."

He looked at me, leaned in and said, "I don't need to. I know what it says. That is their philosophy, not mine."

With that he turned and walked away. I called and got the manager's name and wrote him a letter explaining what had happened. Until this day, I have not heard from that manager. No wonder Mike was the way he was. His behavior was consistent with what management allowed him to be.

Last year a group I was speaking for held their meeting

in that hotel. I told them I wouldn't stay there. I explained the situation and told them "I refuse to stay where my presence is not appreciated as a customer."

I stayed next door and had a great experience. At that property they saw the guest as an asset, not an interruption. Their behavior said, "We want you to come back!" Customer Care is a behavior, not a concept. Until companies realize this, they will continue to put people in places whose presence is about frustrating the customer, but not making them excited about coming back.

I wrote this chapter while on a Delta flight from Atlanta to Norfolk. My seatmate was this young lady who I kept watching read what I was writing. When I closed my computer, she asked me, "What are you doing?"

"I'm writing a book on customer care."

"Sounds interesting. I wish our company would read it."

"Why?"

"We preach customer care, but really don't care about it. I am the Customer Service person. My job is to make sure we are delivering the best possible service to our customers. It is really a joke. I bring issues to management and they just look at me, shrug and never address it."

"Why do you stay?"

"I was with the company they bought. I have a few years left and I can retire. I don't want to walk away now."

"Doesn't the fact they don't care bother you?"

"Bother me! I get upset everyday. I hear all the war stories from our customers. I watch us lose business. In the old company we were the service leaders. We were known for our quality care. This company is only interested in making money. As long as they can show a profit, they don't care about anything else."

There was this long pause as she stared out the window. "We are the top company in our industry. We could be so much better. I just wish we cared more about our customers. Oh well, I just have a few more years and I am out of there."

Isn't it a shame how companies care about their customers when they need them, BUT when they don't need them, their behavior is one that sends a negative message to the customer.

Customer Care Questions:
- *Do you work for a company that really cares about its customers?*
- *Do you see ways customer care could be improved?*
- *What would be the first improvement you think should be made?*

What Is Taking Care Of The Customer All About?
S   satisfaction is the driving force
E   environment is always customer friendly
R   responding, not reacting to customer concerns
V   vision is shared by all
I   investigating to make sure care is happening
C   confusion handled before it is a problem
E   expectations met

I Can Fix It With My Hammer
Be careful what you say; the customer is listening.

Have you ever overheard a conversation you were not supposed to hear?

All of us have dreams. For some their dream gets buried. It doesn't mean it is not there; it is just buried under all the clutter in their life. The more clutter in your life, the more challenging it is for you to see and/or focus on your dream. A dream is something you have to feed every day with positive behavior. It is the action that determines whether the dream lives or dies.

For years, I had a dream of owning a Rolls Royce Corniche. I remember the first time I went to the Rolls Dealership in the Palm Beaches. I walked around with my imagination running wild. I would look at the price tags and dream of the day when I could afford that car.

On one of my visits I met Gordon Hunter. Gordon was not just another car salesperson; he was someone who cared. We sat and talked and I told him about my dream. He smiled and I knew he understood the mission I was on. He said, "Richard, I will help you fulfill your dream."

I knew he meant it. I knew he was placed in my life to help me make this a reality. About four months after that conversation he called me. "Richard, I have your car."

"You what?" I said in a voice filled with surprise and excitement.

"I have your car. How fast can you get down here? I have your name on it, but it won't last long."

I was off the phone, flew out the door and flying to the Rolls Dealership. When I arrived, Gordon was waiting.

Information that creates
fear for the customer is
going to make it challenging
to satisfy them.

"Come on. I think you are really going to like this car."

I walked out to the lot and there was this beautiful royal blue Rolls Royce Corniche. I stopped dead in my tracks and just stared at it. It was exactly what I had been looking for.

"Go ahead," Gordon said. "You can touch it, feel it, sit in it and drive it."

"Where did you find this?"

"It was part of a gentleman's estate. He bought it for his wife as a gift and she hated it. It has been parked in their garage. When he died recently, they brought it to us to sell."

He paused and just watched me stare at the car. "It is a 1985 with only 21,000 miles on it. It is in mint condition. Richard, this is a very rare find."

I walked over and looked at that car from the top to the bottom. He said, "Get in. This is what you have been dreaming about. Get in. Don't just stand there with your mouth open. Get in and let's take it for a drive."

I took that car for a drive and it was great. Back at the dealership we worked out all the details and I left with my dream being fulfilled. What a great feeling. Imagine, for ten years you have had this dream. Each day you invest your efforts into creating a journey to make it come true. Each week you move with a purpose and that purpose continues to push you to continue to move toward the achievement of that dream.

The consistency of action makes this more than a wish. A wish is something you think about, but emotionally doubt you can ever have. A dream is something you think about and mentally know it is possible. This had been my dream for ten years, and now it was reality.

For a month I would get up every morning, go out and

remove every speck of dust from that car. It didn't matter that it stayed in the garage. It didn't matter every night I would wipe it down. I just wanted to touch it. This was a dream come true.

I had the car for about a year when Karen and I built our home in Newport News, Virginia. We sold the house in South Florida and had to move the Rolls to Virginia. I didn't want to drive it that far. Truth is, I didn't want to put that many miles on it. In that year, I had only put about 300 miles on it.

We searched and found a trucking company that majored in moving cars like the Rolls. I checked them out from A to Z. Everything said they would treat my car like I treated it.

It was a Thursday when the truck pulled up in front of the house in Virginia. I was on the road when they picked it up in Florida, but Karen had slowly walked me through each step they went through in loading it. Did you know they wrapped the car in clear plastic wrapping?

I watched as they lowered the tailgate of that enclosed carrier and there was my dream. The driver backed it off, placed it in the driveway and said to me. "Mr. Flint, we had to move the cars around to make a delivery and in the process there was some damage to the undercarriage. The protective wire netting got slightly bent."

Well, I want to tell you my heart stopped! All I heard was "there was some damage to the car." I must have turned white. The driver looked at me and continued. "It really isn't anything major. It just needs to be adjusted. Have it fixed and let us know the cost, and we will pay for it."

It didn't matter whether it was anything serious; that was my ten-year dream he was talking about. He walked me over and showed me what he was talking about. He was right; it was nothing serious. The wire mesh that covered some of the undercarriage was bent.

I immediately searched the Yellow Pages for a Rolls Royce dealership in the area and to my surprise the closest one was in Bethesda, Maryland. That was a three-hour journey from Newport News. I called Euro Motors and asked them about someone in the area who they would recommend. I talked with Steve, and he told me about a gentleman in Virginia Beach who used to work for them. He was certified to work on the car. I called and made an appointment to take the car for him to look at.

When I arrived at his Body Shop, I thought I was at the wrong place. The front looked like a junkyard with old broken down cars sitting everywhere.

I got out, walked in and was greeted by two of the biggest dogs you have ever seen. I had to fight my way through them to get to the counter where this young lady was watching me push through. She laughed and said, "Don't worry about them. They are harmless; they just love people."

I told her I was there to see Ray. "He is busy at this minute. Have a seat and he will be with you in a few minutes. I walked over to the couches she pointed to, took one look and decided I didn't want to sit there. They were covered in dog hair. In fact those two huge dogs beat me to the couch and took over. I couldn't have sat there if I had wanted to.

In a few minutes Ray came out. "You must be the guy with the Rolls. Tell me what you need."

"I just had the car shipped here from Florida and in the process they bent the wire mesh over part of the undercarriage."

"Let's see what they did."

We walked out to the car; he bent down and looked at

the mesh. "Let me get Guy who would be the one to fix this. Hang on a minute."

He disappeared into the shop and soon reappeared with this huge man who had large greasy hands. He walked over to the car and laid his greasy hand on the fender as he bent down to look at the wire mesh.

He got back up, walked over to where Ray was standing and in a whisper said, "I can fix that. All I got to do is take a hammer and beat it out."

Now, he didn't know I was listening. I heard every word he said — especially the part about a hammer and beating it out. You can imagine the emotions that went through me. Here was my ten-year dream and a man talking about taking a hammer and hitting my car with it.

Ray walked back over, looked at me and said, "No problem. Guy says he can fix it. Now, one more question. Who is going to pay for this? Are you paying for it or the insurance company?"

"Why is that important," I said not understanding the purpose of the question.

"Well, it will be more if the insurance company pays for it."

That was all I needed to hear. First, there were the dogs, next the hammer and finally a very unethical statement.

I looked at Ray and said, "I need to think this through. Would you have Guy get a clean rag and wipe his greasy hand print off my car?"

He looked at me with a strange look, motioned to Guy to wipe the fender and said, "We can do it right away."

All I could see was Guy with this big hammer hitting my car. "No, I think I need to wait."

I got back in my car and drove back home. All I could think about was the hammer. I thought to myself *be careful what you say; the customer may be listening.*

I called Euro Motors and arranged for them to come pick up my car. I don't know how they fixed the car, BUT no one mentioned a hammer to me.

There is so much to be said about how information is presented to the customer. Information that creates fear for the customer is going to be interrupted in a negative fashion. That will chase the customer off. The presentation of information should be to calm the customer, so they will be open to hearing what is being said. Fear of what is going to happen will cause the customer to question how things are going to be done. That will make it challenging to satisfy the customer. One of the beginning aspects of delivering quality customer care is to take the fear from the customer's experience. A calm customer is much easier to work with.

Customser Care Questions:
- *Have you ever had the words of a service person frighten you?*
- *What would you have done in the above situation?*
- *Are you good at taking customer fear away?*

How Do You Take The Customer's Fear Away?
F   find out what they see as their need
E   emotionally feel where they are
A   address each issue through knowledge
R   respond calmly to every question

You Matter
The number one thing a human wants to know is they matter.

Our world has become so impersonal. It seems many businesses have created ways to make sure their people don't have to deal with another human.

Not too long ago when you pulled into a filling station, they came out to pump your gas, clean your windshield and check your oil. Now, they talk to you through an intercom from bulletproof glass.

At one time you could call a company and talk to a human. Now, you call many companies and you get an automated receptionist that sends you through a menu you are not prepared for. You get through the menu, and if you can remember what was said, you push a number to get through to a person's voice mail. So much for personal attention.

I find the entire issue between the airlines and the travel agencies to be intriguing. The travel agency was there as a business partner with the airlines. They could control the lines at the airport with the help of the travel agent. Then, the airlines decided they didn't need the travel agent. They could cut out their business partner and force the customer to go to the Internet or through their own reservation people. Interesting concept! What has happened is a customer that is even more confused dealing with reservation people who are not well trained, sitting in a phone center somewhere in the world, and handling people like cattle.

Go to the airport and try to get a ticket. First, if you are not traveling on that day, there are only certain hours they will sell you a ticket. If you are traveling on that day, the lines are so long and the counter people so frustrated, they treat you like

It is easier for most companies to punish their customers, than face their internal people issues.

the enemy when you tell them you need to purchase the ticket.

Karen went to the Delta counter at Patrick Henry Airport to pick up some tickets. We tried to do it through the travel agency, but the agency was told because we were using vouchers the airline had given us, the tickets had to be purchased at the airport. She arrived and told the agent she wanted to purchase a ticket for herself, for me and one other staff person. The agent looked at her, looked at the vouchers and told her she couldn't purchase Clarita's ticket or mine. We had to be there in person.

Karen has traveled enough to know what is right and what is wrong. She knew what she was told was not correct. When she questioned the young man at the counter, he got upset with her persistency. She left frustrated and without the tickets.

I arrived back home the next morning and together we went to the Delta counter at Patrick Henry Airport. Again, there was the same agent standing in front of us. I explained what I wanted to do, handed him a copy of the flight schedule and the vouchers from Delta Airlines. The look on his face told me *he was in over his head.* He stood there with the information and his computer. He worked for a moment, excused himself and came back with another person.

He looked at Karen and me and said, "I'm sorry. I am new and haven't done this before."

I know Karen well enough to know she was fuming inside. We walked down the counter and she looked at me with fire in her eyes.

"I knew he didn't know what he was doing. Why couldn't he just tell me he didn't know how to do the tickets, rather than making me feel I was wrong? How can they put people on the counter who can't do what they are there to do?"

We went back to the counter and waited as they both worked on the tickets. Two of the tickets they worked out. The third one, which was Karen's ticket, was a different story.

Brad looked at us and asked, "Do you know how they got this fare?"

"No idea. The agency put it together with Delta and this was the fare we were given."

"I cannot get this fare. It comes up higher. Hang on a minute."

He disappeared into the back room and after about fifteen minutes came back to the counter. "I have been on the phone with reservations and they cannot figure where this fare came from. The fare we are getting is $75 higher. I'm sorry, but that is what we are going to have to charge."

We wrote him a check for Karen's ticket, left, went back to the office and called the agency. I explained to Aylin what had happened and she was totally confused.

"Delta made the reservation. That is not our fare. It is the fare Delta gave us. Let me call Delta and see what is going on."

About an hour later she calls me back and says, "Those people at the airport messed up. The fare I gave you is correct. Besides, they changed Karen's class of service and took away her right to upgrade with you. It has taken Beverly and me an hour to get it all straight with Delta. The good news is they overcharged you. The bad news is you are going to have to go back to the airport and have them reissue the ticket. They are the only ones who can correct this."

So, Karen and I make our way back to the airport, back to the Delta ticket counter to once again purchase a ticket. We explain to the young lady at the counter what has happened and the look on her face told us she had no idea what we were talking about.

She said, "Just a minute." She disappeared into the back room and returned with Brad who was puzzled to see us.

"Brad, I went back and called the agency to see what had happened. They called Delta and the fare we gave you this morning was correct. It should all be stored in your records."

The look on his face told us he was just as confused as us. "I called central reservations and they are the ones who told me they could not find the fare you had. I don't understand what is happening."

We stood there for another thirty minutes while Brad and the station manager tried to figure out how to redo the ticket they had already done. All of this because the airline, through its bottom line greed mentality, had decided to no longer use its business partner to help the customer. All of this because Delta, like most companies, is more interested in saving a buck than making sure the customer has a hassle free experience. All of this because those who were there to help, didn't know what they were doing. Rather than Franklin telling Karen he didn't know how to do what she was asking, he punished her by making her feel she was wrong. All he had to tell her was, "I am the only one here and I don't know how to do this. I hate to ask you, but would you mind coming back in the morning when someone will be here who can help you."

Know what? She would have respected that and been happy to come back, BUT he didn't treat her by respecting her time. He didn't make her feel like she mattered. She left as a frustrated customer who went to the airport to simply purchase three airline tickets. Doesn't mesh with their slogan *Delta is ready when you are.* They are ready, but not to take care of you. They are ready to make sure you have a hassle filled experience.

It seems easier for companies to put walls in place to shield their people from their customers, than it is to address the people issues within their company. It is easier to punish the customers than resolve their own people challenges.

Don't these companies realize what they are doing? Aren't they paying attention to the punishment they are handing out to the customer? Don't they understand *the #1 thing the customer wants to know is they matter?*

I think the bottom line truth is *they simply don't care.* If they cared, they would treat the customer with respect. You can't tell me companies don't know their customer connection points that create confusion for the customer. You can't tell me they can't resolve the issues that consistently punish the customer. The reality is *they just don't care.* What matters are their checkbooks, not the customer. Someone needs to remind them *the customer also has a checkbook.*

Customer Care Questions:
- *Have you tried to do business with a company and found it challenging to talk to a human?*
- *Do you think most people still want to do business with a live person?*
- *Have you had to work with someone whose behavior told you they didn't care?*

How Do You Tell A Customer They Matter?

M	make a fuss over them
A	address all concerns quickly
T	talk with them, not at them
T	take their issues seriously
E	expectations agreed to and met
R	refuse to let them leave confused

HELP!
Never make the customer feel like an intrusion.

How many times have you gone into a store, had a question and not been able to find someone to help you? When you walked in, there were people everywhere, but the minute you had a question, they were all gone.

How many times have you found someone, asked them a question and been told where to go? You follow their instructions and still cannot find what you are looking for.

This has been one of the things that impressed me about Wal-Mart. When Sam Walton was alive, his commitment was to making the customer's experience as hassle free as possible. He wanted the customer to feel appreciated and satisfied. That is why the greeters at the front door were so important. When you entered, they were there with their smile and their simple question — *May I help you find anything?* That was so important. You felt like family the minute you walked in. If you were looking for something and couldn't find it, you could ask any Wal-Mart person and they would take you there. They didn't point; they guided. They made sure you were taken care of.

Lately, I have noticed all that has changed. I have been in several Wal-Marts where there were no greeters. I have asked for help and had the person point me in the direction. I guess Sam's death changed the way the new people handle Sam's beliefs.

When Home Depot first came on the scene, they were very customer friendly. You could ask any of the Home Depot people for information, and they would take you to the aisle that contained what you needed. Recently, I have seen that

When the customer doesn't matter to the company, the company won't matter to the customer.

change. I have been in several Home Depots where they simply point. I guess when you get successful, you change some of the practices that made people appreciate being there.

Each time the customer feels lost, they need help. Each time the customer has a question, they need to know someone cares enough to answer their question. When the customer has to ask for help and can't get an answer, they question the business they are doing with the company.

There have been many companies that started with the right design. They build their reputation on taking care of the customer. Then, when they have tasted success and are profitable, it is okay to change the design. The tragic part of this is the number of these companies that simply forgot the reason they got into the business of customer care. It was to connect a product the customer needed to the need the customer had. Their people were there to make the connection a pleasant experience and create an environment where the customer wanted to come back. The result of them forgetting their real purpose is they are no longer in business or no longer profitable. They may want to blame the customer, but this is not the customer's fault. They forgot the mission of customer care.

You cannot punish the customer and continue to grow. At some point, it will catch up with you. The message is very simple. *Upset your customer enough times and they will make your competition very successful.*

One day I needed to purchase some sheets and towels for an apartment I was furnishing. There was a Sears store in the local mall, so I decided to go there. I knew they would have what I needed. I arrived at the store, found the bed sheets and began to search for the right size. I found everything, except what I needed. I looked up and saw this Sears employee coming toward me.

As he approached, I said, "Can you help me?"

He looked at me, looked at his watch and replied, "I am on break."

With that, he just walked on by. Know what I did? I turned, walked out of the store and I have never been back to a Sears store since. When those who are there to help are too busy to take the time to help, the customer understands they don't matter.

The customer care principle is simple. *Never make the customer feel like an intrusion.* When the customer feels unappreciated, the experience will always be viewed as negative. When the experience is perceived as negative, the company has wasted the money it has spent getting the customer through the door.

Again, companies need to understand their mission is not to get the customer through the door, but to create such a positive experience they want to come back and do more business with them. That door is created by any and all connection points with those who represent the company.

It can be the receptionist. How important is that person who answers the company phones? I think they are a critical front line person. Yet, many companies make this one of the lowest paid people on their staff.

Someday when you have a few minutes pick up the phone and call Gateway Title Insurance in Independence, Ohio. When you do, you will meet Debbie. Debbie is one of the best receptionists I have ever met. There is energy in her voice; there is the desire to help the person calling; there is patience in how she deals with people. She is there as a definition of

Gateway's commitment to quality customer care.

Put that in contrast with the company I called in Anchorage, Alaska. I was returning their phone call. The phone rings four times and I am greeted by their receptionist with these words. "What the hell do you want?"

My response was, "Not to talk to you."

"I'm sorry. I am not having a good day."

"Thanks for taking your day out on me."

Do you think I created a perception of that company? Why can't companies understand the importance of the customer connection points?

That door is created by the appearance of the people who represent the company. I think the business world has become too casual in its business dress. I don't think you have to always wear your Sunday best, but there is such a thing as business casual. One lady put it this way. "I want to be helped, not shocked."

That is a good way to state it. Clothes should be clean and pressed. Appearance should be neat. Hair should be combed and facial hair on men trimmed. One should look like they spent time getting ready for work, not jumping out of bed and just made it to work.

That door is created by the appearance of the store. Have you ever walked through a store that was so cluttered you had to fight your way through? When the customer has to struggle to get to what they want, they will chose to not fight and go somewhere that is ready for their arrival.

That door is created by the appearance of the equipment the company uses. For years, Dale and Darlene Travis were in the home restoration and remodeling business. I appreciated Dale's commitment to the appearance of his trucks. I asked him one day, "Why is the appearance so important to you."

He looked at me and smiled. "Those trucks are part of our reputation. When people are paying you to work inside their house and you drive up in a dirty truck, they think that is the way you are going to treat their house. If you show up in a clean truck and the person who represents you is neat, they tend to relax and trust how you are going to do the job."

There is a lot of truth and wisdom in his thinking. People don't just pay for a product; they are buying the experience. That experience is created by all the people they have to go through to get their need resolved.

I think it is safe to say the door that will bring them back is created by:

- attitude
- appearance
- presentation
- behavior

These four form the foundation of perception. How important is that perception? Many times, it is the determining factor whether you are a one-time experience in their life or they become your customer.

Don't forget, your peoples':

- Attitude demonstrates their true desire;
- Appearance states their respect for what they are doing;
- Presentation shows their commitment;
- Behavior never lies.

How important are these four traits in building customers who are committed to repeat and referral business?

Customer Care Questions:
- *Do you agree work dress has become too casual?*
- *Do you agree total appearance makes a statement about customer commitment?*
- *Could your company do a better job of taking care of the customer once they come through the door?*

What Does That Customer Door Represent?
D   decisions customer will make
O   opportunity to create customer loyalty
O   opportunities that didn't exist
R   repeat and referral business

I HATE CUSTOMERS!
*Never keep people who don't care about the customer's
experience.*

Say it any way you want to say it. Explain it any way
you want to explain it. The truth is quality customer care
comes down to people taking care of people. When people in
the service sector do a good job of taking care of those who are
seeking to fulfill a need, quality service has taken place.

When people in the service sector don't do a quality job
of taking care of those who are seeking to fulfill a need, quality
service has not happened.

As difficult as many make it sound, it is really very
simple. When quality people do a quality job of customer care,
there is not a customer care issue.

Why is that so challenging for those who lead
companies to understand? If you place your emphasis on
people taking care of people, profit will be made.

Why is it so challenging for management to
understand? You hire people to accept the responsibility of
taking care of YOUR customers. You make it clear that is their
purpose in being there. If they don't do it, they don't stay.

Write the expectations concerning customer care,
explain the expectations governing the behavior for customer
care and hold people to the mission of taking care of the
customer. It's as simple as it sounds!

What makes that so challenging to achieve? Here are
some of the reasons why, I think, we are facing the issue of the
lack of customer care.

First, *management is afraid of losing people.* This is
huge. It is not the fact they don't know they have people who

Customer Service is
simply people taking care
of people!

don't care. The truth is they are fearful of losing people and having to replace them. That means those who don't care are guiding the business environment.

Any time you are fearful of losing someone, they emotionally own the environment. They know you don't want to lose them. They know they can break the rules without suffering any consequences; they know management won't do anything. Put this together and you have an unfriendly customer environment.

One manager of a department said it this way. "If I get rid of those who don't care, I am just going to end up hiring more just like them. That means investing time and energy in training people like the ones I already have. What is the sense? They may not be the best, but are as good as what is out there."

That is sad commentary coming from one who has been given the responsibility of designing the customer care environment.

Another reason the issue exists is *management has grown tired of fighting what they feel is a losing battle.*

One manager said this to me. "You have no idea how much money we have spent on customer service programs. We have made it our top priority and we keep the issue at the forefront of all our meetings. Reality is, we aren't doing any better. In fact, if the truth were known, we are probably doing worse. I am just so tired of fighting this battle over customer care."

He paused, looked around to make sure no one was listening and continued. "I'll be real honest with you. I've given up hoping we are ever going to improve. I just try to keep the jungle as calm as possible. I am really tired of fighting this battle."

If the truth was known, this manager was simply stating what most in management are feeling. They are tired of beating their head against a brick wall with people who don't care. For them it has become easier to fight the fires from the customers, than fight the battle with their people. What a tragic commentary.

Another reason this issue exists is *the lack of people skills training within the management ranks.* Yes, companies do some form of training, but not for the people skills management needs. They train on product knowledge, computer skills, budgeting, controlling inventory and other product driven needs. I am not saying these are not important, BUT they are missing an important ingredient. They are not educating management in the art of understanding people.

You don't manage products! You manage people. You order products, produce products, warehouse products, inventory products; you don't manage products. You manage people.

One young manager stated it this way. "I came to work for this company because they promised me management training. Right now, I am very disappointed in the management training. I can control inventory, write an order, use the computer and talk about our products. What I can't do is manage people. I feel like they want me to manage the intangibles. That is not what is going to help us improve. If we are to become the better company they keep preaching, we are going to have to do a better job of managing people. That is where our issues lie. Hey, we have the products; we just don't have the right people."

He paused, scratched his head and looked at me with a frown on his face. "I told my boss about this one guy who spends most of his time talking on his cell phone. I wanted to let him go and was told I couldn't. My boss told me the guy may not be the best, but at least he shows up. Yeah, he shows up, but doesn't do anything. I watched him ignore a customer the other day because he was on his phone. I wanted to fire him right then, but I knew I would be in trouble if I did. His behavior isn't right, and we tolerate it. That's not right either. We must stop making excuses for these people and let managers manage. Give us the training to be better at our job. Give us the authority to do what we know should be done. Stop telling us we are managers when we are not skilled and not trusted to make the right decisions."

He is right! If people in service positions don't care about taking care of the customer, they should be gotten rid of. What kind of a message is being sent through the ranks when a company preaches customer service and then, makes excuses for those who don't care about customer care?

Most managers don't refer to themselves as a manager. They refer to themselves as "babysitters." They come in everyday to the adult day care and try to keep the customers from killing the employees. They work to keep the flames of discontent as low as they can. Management has become a thankless job filled with unrealistic expectations designed by upper management whose only concern is producing a good balance sheet for the stockholders.

If you are going to call these people "managers," train them to manage. Give them the people skills to deal with the people issues. Once they are trained, trust their decision-making and let them do what needs to be done to improve the company's presence with the customers.

Another reason this issue exists is *many in management*

have stopped having fun. They have become like so many in the workforce who show up each day for the paycheck.

They have a JOB! Remember my definition of a JOB? It is an environment where one goes each day and prostitutes their self for a paycheck.

Many managers are tired, frustrated, overwhelmed, resentful, bored and just flat out not enjoying what they are doing. Rather than their career being a mission, it has deteriorated to simply being a job. Now, do you think that affects their caring process? Do you think they emotionally become a person that goes through a routine?

People who are having fun want to make a difference. People who are having fun want to be part of an environment that is making a difference. People who are having fun make it possible for others to have fun.

I had finished my program at the National Association of Convenience Stores and was packing up things when this gentleman approached. I looked at him and he had the biggest smile on his face.

My program was about enjoying what you have chosen to do with your life. He looked at me and said, "Boy, are you right! What you say may not be popular, but you really make people face themselves. You are right on with what you say."

He stopped, smiled and then, laughed out loud. "I have said for years if you can't have fun doing what you are doing, you shouldn't be doing it. Life is way too short to spend your time doing anything that doesn't bring joy to your life. I left the last job I had because it just stopped being fun. I left behind a lot of people who are just hanging out in their job waiting for the day to come when they either win the lottery or can retire. Just think what those people are doing to all the lives they come in contact with. No wonder we are having so much trouble with customer service."

When management is not having fun, it is a good bet those in the workforce will reap the behaviors that go with their leader not enjoying what they are doing.

Several years ago, I was having a President's Conference at a Golf Resort in Miami. It was the morning of the third day and we were all in the restaurant trying to have breakfast. We had been seated for several minutes and still had not been served any coffee. We looked around and yes, the restaurant was crowded, but there were plenty of servers to handle the number of people who were there. One of the Company Presidents at my table said with a smirk on his face, "Not a good example of taking care of the customer. I think I will get us some coffee."

He got up, went to the coffee station, returned with a pot of coffee and poured it for us. Two servers were standing at the corner having a conversation and watching him pour the coffee. They didn't bother to come over and finish what he had started. He returned the coffee pot to the station, returned to the table and said, "Interesting!" as he watched the two servers look at him and then turn back to their conversation.

The two servers who had been watching were talking loud enough we could hear them. One looked at us, turned back to the other and said in a very sarcastic tone, "I will be glad when these damn customers leave. I am tired and don't feel like having to wait on them today."

The President who had served the coffee looked at me and said, "So far they haven't served us. Do me a favor? Don't ever bring us back here again. They don't appreciate our business, and with this attitude I don't want to give them any business."

To make matters worse there was an automatic gratuity of 18% added to the check. I took the check, scratched it out and put a zero in its place.

After the conclusion of the conference, I asked to meet with the management staff. I walked them through the experience. The restaurant manager looked at the group, shook his head and replied to my concern with, "I know we have a problem. We have been working on it, but we are short handed and cannot afford to make any changes. We are going to have to tolerate this for a little longer."

How dangerous was his statement? How much damage can these people do to the customer wanting to come back? The hotel property has been a great resort, one of my favorite in the USA, but when the people who are there to take care of the customer don't care, the quality of the rest of the resort's amenities are devalued.

It didn't matter if they were short staffed, the server should have been fired. Rather than her manager making an excuse for her behavior, he should have heard the seriousness of the concerns of my people and took immediate action. The lack of action validated her behavior. The rule should be a principle that is never compromised. *Never keep people who don't care about the customer's experience.*

Customer Care Questions:
- *Do you agree that the real issue in most companies is the lack of quality management?*
- *Should people who demonstrate a lack of customer care be fired?*
- *Does the customer have the right to expect quality customer care?*

The Responsibility Of Management In Making Sure Customer Care Happens:

    C   confront any person who is not customer driven

    A   address all customer concerns quickly

    R   refuse to accept anything less than quality

    E   eliminate those who don't care

SHOW ME THE MONEY
*People either spend or buy; the difference is defined by the
quality of the service they receive.*

Money is power! Money in the hands of the consumer
is even more powerful. When the consumer decides to spend
money, they express their power. When the consumer decides
not to spend money, they make a statement about their power.

Money can be a weapon. If there is one thing
companies listen to, it is when the consumer withdraws their
dollars. As long as the consumer is spending dollars and
buying products, companies think they are doing okay. Let
the consumer withdraw their dollars and watch the panic
companies go through.

It's interesting to study the power of the dollar. It's
confusing trying to understand why companies don't get it. If
they take care of their customers, their customers will take care
of them. If they neglect taking care of their customers, their
customers will go away and take their dollars with them.

Sometimes you feel companies think the consumer is
stupid. They develop the attitude that the consumer needs them
more than they need the consumer. The consumer can feel that
attitude each time they try to do business with the company.
The forgotten part of this thought process is *the consumer
holds the future of the company in their wallets.*

What the consumer expects from the company is their
needs met by the people who are there to help them, not being
hassled by the people the company put in front of them to take
care of their need. There are always other companies selling
the same product the customer needs. For any company to
think they are the one and only place for the customer to

The customer's checkbook is what they use to define how good you are at customer care!

go is out of touch with reality. Daily, customers prove this by driving past stores that carry what they need to go to a place where their needs are met and they have a hassle free experience.

Let me go back for a minute and talk about this thing called money. Everyday people use money to achieve two things:

- *solutions to a need*
- *good feelings*

Most companies place their emphasis on their ability to meet the customer's need. They understand the concept of creating an environment that is customer friendly, but that is secondary to meeting the customer's product need. The result is they are only focusing on one aspect of customer care.

The customer has a product/service need, but that is not as important to them as entering an environment that is customer friendly. They understand they can go several places and have their product needs met and are not opposed to doing that.

If companies were really into customer satisfaction, wouldn't they put their emphasis on customer friendly environments, rather than just selling them a product?

If companies were really into customer care, wouldn't they do a better job of monitoring the quality of the environment the customer is walking into?

One thing I have learned from traveling as much as I do is *no matter what they say about the strength of luggage, an airline can destroy any piece at any given time.* Have you ever watched those baggage handlers do their job of *handling* luggage? Many do a good job, but there are those who see a piece of luggage as the enemy that must be destroyed.

One time on an American Airline flight, I was waiting for my suitcase to appear. Now, if you travel, you understand the emotions you go through standing there watching the belt start, the luggage going around and everyone has theirs - except you. When it is not there, you are now faced with the trauma that goes with facing that person in Baggage Service. You know who gets that job, don't you? The person who is being punished. As much as you don't want to face them, they don't want to face you. I have spent years studying the look on their face as you approach the Baggage Service office. It is enough to make you forget your luggage and run.

Oh well, back to my American Airline flight. The baggage belt did its thing and after several minutes, my bag appeared. The challenge was it didn't appear as I expected it to. The bag was open and there were clothes hanging out. I took it off the belt and started checking to make sure everything was there. When I looked for my shoes, I noticed a pair of blue shoes was missing. For some reason I looked up and, behold, coming down the belt was one blue shoe. I picked it up and waited for its mate to come along. Well, it never appeared. I took my bag and my one shoe to Baggage Service where I came face-to-face with Phil.

Now, Phil was an interesting person. He had a huge amount of chewing gum in his mouth. I watched as he punished the people in front of me. You could tell his level of frustration by watching the intensity of his gum chewing. The higher his frustration, the stronger his chewing.

Finally, it was my time. I walked up to the counter, put my one blue shoe on the counter and looked at him.

He looked at the shoe, looked at me and said with this look of confusion on his face. "Can I help you?"

"Phil," I said. "When I checked my luggage in Ontario, I had two blue shoes packed in my suitcase, and when I arrived here in Dallas, I had one blue shoe come down the baggage belt. This shoe is lonely for its mate."

"Are you sure you packed both shoes? Maybe you left one where you came from."

"Phil, my shoes travel in pairs. When I left the hotel with my luggage, there were two blue shoes. When I checked my luggage at the airport, there were two blue shoes in my bag. When I arrived here in Dallas, my luggage came out opened and one blue shoe is all that arrived. What can we do to find his friend?"

The look on his face said, "I don't have time for this." He picked up the phone, called the baggage service area that handled my flight, chatted for a minute and then came back to me with this blank look on his face. "Well, they tell me all the luggage is off the plane. They are going to look in the baggage bin and call me back. Have a seat. They should call me back shortly."

Now, if I had been smart, I would have asked, "What does shortly mean?" I took a seat and waited. I got tired of sitting, so I got up and walked around. After thirty minutes I went back to Phil and asked, "Phil, do you think they have had time to check the plane's baggage area by now?"

He looked up from what he was doing and said, "You have to be patient. They are busy out there." With that, he looked back down as his way of dismissing me.

I was patient for another twenty-five minutes. "Phil," I said in a much stronger voice. "I have been patient for almost an hour. I need to get to the hotel and get ready for my presentation. Would you call and see what they found out about my shoe?"

He pushed his work aside, looked at me with eyes that told me "go to hell," picked up the phone and called. He didn't say much, hung up the phone and said, "No shoe."

He reached for a form and we started the process of gathering information. "Okay," he said. "What does the shoe look like?"

I slowly moved the lonely blue shoe toward him and said, "It looks like this one, only it goes on my left foot."

He picked up the shoe, looked at it and said, "Nice shoes! I bet they cost a lot. I need to know their value."

"$800 dollars."

"Now, that's for both of them, so that would be $400 for one."

The look on my face must have startled him. "Phil, we are talking about a pair of shoes, not just one shoe. I need both of them to wear as a pair."

He marked out $400 and replaced it with $800. He finished and told me they would call me when and if they found the shoe.

That was three years ago and I haven't seen my one blue shoe. For four months, I called trying to find out what American Airlines was going to do about replacing my shoes. Each time I would call, I was handed from person-to-person, and each time I had to tell the story all over again. Each time I was told someone would get back to me, but there were no phone calls.

Finally, I was paid for the shoe. The challenge was what I had to go through to resolve a situation I didn't create, but seemed to be punished for. I was simply a customer trying to resolve an issue I didn't create, but was made to feel I was responsible for. The loss of the shoe was an opportunity for American Airlines to demonstrate how important I was as a customer. Instead, they made it an arena where I felt like the enemy.

I have never forgotten the way I was treated. Since that time, I have refused to spend my travel dollars with American Airlines. It didn't matter to them that, for several years, I had spent an average of $20,000 a year with them. I was just another inconvenience Phil had to deal with. Why would I want to spend money with an airline that made me feel like the enemy when the situation was one they created?

Companies need to constantly remind themselves of the power the consumer has with their dollars. Each day they either spend or buy. The difference is created by the people they have to go through to fulfill their need. If their experience is positive and they feel good about what has happened, they will continue to buy and buy and buy. If their experience is not positive and they feel they don't matter, they spend their dollars and then go looking for a company that appreciates their business.

Taking care of the customer is a commitment that must be made by all the people who represent the company. A company is not a product; a company is an environment that is either healthy or unhealthy. The company doesn't get to define which one they are; the customer makes that decision and defines it with their dollars. Do you think the customer can make a powerful statement with their dollars?

Customer Care Questions:
- *Do you understand the difference between spending and buying?*
- *Have you ever stopped doing business with a company because of the lack of respect they showed you?*
- *Do you think the average company really cares about what the customer feels?*

What Really Makes People Buy, Not Just Spend Money With A Company?

P   people they have to go through
E   emotions that are involved
O   others opinions and experiences
P   personal definition of their experience
L   level of care demonstrated by people
E   expectations and what happens with them

You're Wrong! We Don't Make Mistakes!
When a company can't admit when they have made a mistake, the customer is made to feel like an idiot.

Have you ever been through a bookstore and seen all the books in the "Dummy" series? There is a Dummy book for almost every issue.

I find the concept interesting. Years ago if you called someone a "dummy," you were insulting them. Now, we use the word and people accept that maybe they are. The one book in this series I haven't seen yet is Customers Are Dummies. I really believe many companies sit in their Board Rooms and talk about how stupid customers are. I think many Board of Directors meet and talk about how the public will accept anything. I think they must laugh and giggle as they talk about the next way they are going to punish the customer.

Take the Oil Companies. How many times has it been announced that OPEC is raising the price on crude oil and instantly the price of gas goes up. Now, you know they have oil in storage tanks that has been sitting there. You know there are tankers that have been loaded and on their way to ports to unload. You know the increase in OPEC prices doesn't affect that oil, but what do they tell us? "They must raise the price because the cost of crude oil has increased."

They must think we are dummies. Then, watch what happens when they reveal their profit statements. Their profits soar. They just hope nothing will be said and they can go their merry way, laughing all the way to the bank while thinking *what a bunch of dummies their customers are.*

I wish our government would get back to being a government "of the people, for the people and by the people,"

The customer is not a dummy;
companies that don't understand
this are the real dummies!

rather than a government "of the special interest groups, for the special interest groups and controlled by the contributions they make to their campaign funds." If customer care was really an important issue, government would understand *the public who they represent, are their customers.* Their customers are not the companies and corporations that look for every way not to pay taxes. Their customers are not the major companies and corporations that line their pockets while taking away from those who work to make them profitable.

The government's customer is the average American citizen who goes to work each day in order to make money to spend and keep the economy growing. Something is wrong when government is more interested in what they are given than in what they are giving. Something is wrong when the average American citizen gives government about forty-nine cents out of every dollar they earn to be wasted on special interest groups, rather than facing the issues of our nation.

Don't get me wrong. I think we have the greatest system in the world, BUT there are too many taking because of greed, rather than giving because they care. Business, no matter how you define it, is about people caring about people and demonstrating that fact through behavior.

I guess government could join Corporate America in writing a chapter in the book, <u>Customers Are Dummies</u>. The message presented is very clear. *These groups don't respect the people who keep them in business.*

Take any of these groups who treat people, their customers, like dummies and try to talk to them about their behavior. Their attitude is "You don't understand. We haven't done anything wrong. We don't make mistakes."

In my business, we do a lot of shipping. We ship

educational tools to the seminar locations where I am speaking; we ship customer orders; we do a lot of shipping. Our primary vendor for over thirty years has been UPS (United Parcel Service). They were dependable, friendly and approachable. Then, a few years ago, they went on strike. I am not sure what happened to their commitment to their customers, but it went south.

After the strike, we started having major issues with their handling of packages. We use a heavy gauge of cardboard boxes for our shipments. It didn't matter how heavy the cardboard gauge was, they managed to damage the box and its contents. We called our boxing vendor and went to an even heavier gauge and they still managed to destroy boxes. It didn't matter if we were shipping packages out or back to us, the boxes looked like they had been thrown, rather than handled.

When we talked to UPS's Customer Service, we were told it had to be the way we were packing the boxes. We were assured that packages were handled with care. If that were true, I would hate to see a package that they didn't care about.

I don't know what happened during their strike, but after it was over the attitude of many of their people went south. Denise, my Director of Products, has shared with me several conversations she has had with those within UPS who are there to help the customer. The behavior of many has become angry, negative, unwilling to help and designed to make the customer feel they don't know what they are talking about.

Recently, we had a customer call to inquire about some charges on her Visa Card. It seemed UPS had picked up three shipments from our office and accounting had charged all three to her account. Only one was hers, but for some unknown reason they decided to charge her card for all of them.

Karen went over all the information and couldn't figure out why our customer got charged for the other people's shipment. Each form had the correct information on it and each form included the method of payment.

Karen explained to the lady she would need to send her credit card statement to UPS to have it settled. Three months went by and Karen receives a call from this same lady asking for our help. For three months, she had been talking to UPS about settling this matter and for three months, she had been getting the run around. Each time she called, she talked to a different person and had to go through the entire situation again. Each time she was told they would check into it and get back to her. She would wait and there would be no reply.

Finally, she had had enough and called to see if there was anything we could do to help. Now, if there is one thing I know about Karen, it is *you don't want to get on the wrong side of her.* When people are disrespectful of people and it involves our reputation, she goes to war.

She asked the lady to fax to her a copy of her credit card bill. Looking at the bill, it was apparent that UPS had made a mistake. It was apparent they had charged her for two other people's shipments. She picked up the phone and called UPS. The first person she talked to informed her, "It was impossible; that couldn't have happened. They don't make mistakes like that."

Well, that didn't sit well with her. She proceeded to ask questions only to discover this person couldn't do anything anyway. Now, he didn't volunteer that information. It only came out after Karen kept challenging his statements. Finally, she got the number of the correct person she would need to talk to.

She made that call and again was informed that couldn't have happened. Karen told them she was sitting, looking at the lady's statement and that it had happened. "They wanted proof!" They didn't want information; "they wanted proof!"

What happens when a company doesn't accept responsibility for their actions? Does that behavior make the customer feel valuable? Do you think that creates the spirit of customer loyalty? Do you think it sends a message that says, "We appreciate your business and will take care of the situation?"

When a company cannot admit when they have made a mistake, the customer is made to feel like an idiot. Genuine customer care is about resolving customer's concerns, not fighting a war with them. No, the customer is not always right, but neither is the company. Mistakes will be made; the issue is how are they handled.

Customer care respects the customer's concerns and works with them to find a resolution. Company arrogance treats the customer like a dummy and punishes the fact they have challenged the behavior of the company. When a company goes to war with their customers, it is a battle they might win, but in the long run THEY LOSE!

Customer Care Questions:
- *Does your company treat customers with respect?*
- *When was the last time you were made to feel like a dummy because you asked a question?*
- *Should companies own up to their mistakes?*

What Behaviors Make The Customer Feel Like An Idiot?

I   ignore their concerns

D   don't listen to what they are trying to say

O   offer reasons, not resolution

I   insist they don't know what they are saying

T   they treat them with disrespect

ROMANCE
Customer care is just another form of romance.

When someone cares, they demonstrate it with their behavior. Would you agree with that? You can watch a couple's behavior around each other and know exactly what their relationship is like.

After speaking for a group in Atlanta, I was standing in my booth when this young couple walked up. We chatted for a few minutes and Mic asked, "What do you see when you look at us?"

I motioned them to come with me to a more private area where we sat down. I looked at them for a few seconds before I responded, "What do you want to know?"

Mic looked at Angie, his wife, and said in a voice filled with nerves, "What do you see when you look at us?"

"I see a young couple who are living two lives. There is the life the two of you present in public and there is the other life which comes out when you are behind closed doors."

I paused to watch the look on their faces. They both turned white, looked at each other and then back to me.

"Do you want me to continue?"

They both nodded yes, but never said a word. They leaned in waiting for me to continue.

"In public the two of you have learned how to play a game that says to others you are okay. When you go home and close the door, the masks come off and the struggles you have take over. If the two of you don't get some help, you won't make it another six months."

I paused again to let them emotionally catch up. "Am I anywhere close to being right?"

When the customer no longer
feels they are appreciated,
they start questioning the
value of the relationship.

Mic's body language changed as he sank back into his chair. "You are right on. How did you know that?"

"Last night the two of you were having dinner at the same restaurant where I was. I was doing my normal thing, watching people. I got caught up in watching the behavior between you. When someone from the group would speak to the two of you, you were full of life and smiles. As soon as they would leave, you would slip back into ignoring each other. It is apparent to me that the romance is gone from your relationship."

Angie looked me square in the eyes and responded, "It has been gone for some time. We have become roommates, not husband and wife."

I looked at Mic and asked, "Can you tell me you are in love with Angie?"

My question took him by surprise and he didn't know what to say. Finally, he looked at her, looked back at me and said, "No! Right now I cannot tell you I am in love with her."

I turned to Angie and asked her, "Can you tell me you are in love with Mic?"

She looked at Mic and as the tears gathered in her eyes, she responded with, "No. I cannot honestly tell you I am in love with him."

Do you think when romance diminishes in a relationship, it affects the caring part? Do you think when a person is no longer "in love" it changes their behavior?

In my years of working with relationships, I have found romance to be one of the most important aspects of any relationship. It's the romance that keeps two people paying attention to each other. It's the romance that keeps two people wanting to be with and around each other. It's romance that brings the strength necessary to face and work through any situation they are handed. When the romance diminishes, so does one of the most important connection points.

Take these thoughts and apply them to the world of customer care. Customer care is just another form of romance. As long as the romance is in place, there is a growing relationship filled with trust, loyalty and the feeling we are in this together.

Take the romance out and you create the emotional space for worry, doubt and uncertainty. What do you think those three emotions can do to the foundation of a relationship?

I think the question needs to be asked of companies, big, medium or small, "Are you in love with your customers?"

If the answer is "no," it will be easy to understand why the company has a challenge building its business through quality customer care.

I think the question needs to be asked to the leadership of companies, "Are you in love with your customers?" Their customers are their people. If the answer is "no," you will quickly understand why there is confusion and turmoil within the company walls concerning quality customer care.

Every human wants to feel the thrill of romance. Every human wants to feel they matter. Every human wants to feel special and that someone cares about them. This is true with family, in business and in doing business with a company. Customer care is really just another form of romance. When the romance is weak, so is the caring for the customer. When a company is no longer in love with its customers, internal or external, the result will be a lack of quality customer care, customer appreciation and customer value.

Romance is about presentation. You can always

see how one person feels about the other through their self-presentation to the other person.

Where there is romance, there is caring. You express your feelings through a presentation that says, "I really care for you." That same fact is true with quality customer care — *isn't it?*

Where there is romance, there is support. Maybe it is not something you are overly excited about doing, but because it is important to them, you support their feelings. The presentation tells the other person "I am here with you." That same fact is true with quality customer care — *isn't it?*

Where there is romance, there is communication. You want to listen; you want to talk; you want to express what you think and how you feel. You understand the negative power of silence. The presentation using words tells the other person "I enjoy listening and sharing with you." The same is true with quality customer care — *isn't it?*

Where there is romance, the other person doesn't question your motives. They know who you are because of how you feel about them. That presentation removes the doubt and takes away the worry. The same is true about quality customer care — *isn't it?*

Romance is about "wanting" more than "needing" someone. When your "need" is the driving force, you only see what that person can do to meet your needs. Their presence is one of satisfying your needs. That doesn't allow you to see the total person - just one aspect of who they are.

When your "want" is the driving force, you see the total person. You see the total value they bring. This expands their presence and allows them to continue to add to your life.

The same is true in the world of customer care. Too

many companies "need" the customer to spend their dollars
with them. When they think about the customer, they do so
with limited imagination. When they see the customer, they do
so through eyes that stare at their pocketbook. This forms their
presentation to the customer. If the customer is a looker or a
shopper, they don't pay as much attention to them. To them
the customer's presence only has value when they are spending
money. If they are not spending money, they don't have any
need for them. This behavior doesn't make the customer feel
valuable or create a desire on the part of the customer to be
loyal.

Need is about *doing what I expect you to do.* It narrows
importance, diminishes value and expresses a lack of quality
caring. That is not customer care.

When you "want" the customer, that is where the love
affair takes place. "Want" sees the total customer. It doesn't
look at them as a moment; it doesn't put limitations on their
presence; it is always searching for other ways to connect and
build a stronger relationship. It is about allowing the customer
to have a total presence. If they want to simply look until they
are sure about their decision, it is okay. If they want to shop
around, it is okay. It sends the message of quality care. That
makes the customer want to be loyal. That is quality customer
care. It is like any great relationship – *when the romance is
a growing part, the relationship just keeps getting stronger
and stronger.* Don't let the customer feel they are no longer
valuable by ceasing to pay attention to them.

Customer Care Questions:
- *Do your customers feel the romance?*
- *Can you honestly say your customers are wanted more than they are needed?*
- *Do you agree this concept of customer service is another form of romance?*

What Says You Are In Love With Your Customers?

L   letting them know your appreciation
O   openingly show respect for them
V   very attentive to their desires
E   experience is positive

The Customer Is Not Always Right!
When the customer is wrong, they should be told so.

How many times have you heard, "The customer is always right!" I am not sure where the idea came from, but it is wrong. I am not sure who thought this would enhance the concept of customer care, but they were wrong. Yet, the teaching has become one of the cornerstones for many companies' teaching of customer service.

The thought is not truth; that is not something that companies should practice; that is a concept that actually destroys the spirit of customer service. There are times when a company should be willing to face their negative customers, explain to them their negative attitude will not be tolerated and be willing to fire them if they don't improve. Reality is, *most companies would rather allow that negative customer to beat their internal customer than stand tall and challenge their behavior.* What kind of a message does that send to the company's people? Does that tell their people "we respect you and will protect you from customer abuse," or does it tell their people "you are not as important as our customers and you will take whatever they give you?"

The customer is not always right! That is a fact, and when they are not, they should be told so. When a company allows the negative behavior of a customer to be okay, they validate their behavior and destroy the positive spirit of their people. That sends a negative message in all directions.

I was doing a program for a major paint company and the subject was <u>Mastering The Art of Bringing The Customer Back</u>. During the presentation, I made the statement "you don't want every person to come back. There are some

137

There are times when
you simply need to fire the
customer!

customers you should take to lunch and order theirs to go."
That brought a chuckle from the audience. They knew the
wisdom behind what I was saying, but the dangerous reality is
most don't fire negative customers; they support their negative
behavior.

After the program I was sitting in the hotel lobby
waiting for my ride to the airport when George approached me.
"I really liked what you said today. In principle I agree with
everything you said."

I smiled at him and responded with, "Thank you. I am
intrigued with your choice of words. What do you mean by *in
principle you agree with everything I said?*"

"Well, when you were talking about negative
customers, one man jumped into my mind. He is the most
negative person I call on. He can never be pleased. He is
always looking for something wrong so he can hammer us for
a financial concession. I don't like calling on him, but he is
constantly calling and demanding I come by. When I get there,
it is just another emotional beating. He is an ugly person."

"Why do you keep him as a customer? He is really not
a customer; he is a problem that keeps affecting your spirit."

"You are right about him affecting my spirit. If I see
him early in the day, the rest of my day is ruined. If I see him
late in the day, I go home an angry person. I have talked to my
boss about him, but all I hear is *he spends money with us. You
just have to tolerate him.* I don't know how much longer I can
tolerate his emotional beatings."

"Have you talked to him about his behavior?"

"Oh, I made that mistake once. One day he pushed me
over the edge, and I let him know about it. I hadn't been out of
his office for more than thirty minutes when I got a call from
my boss. He wanted to know what I had done to upset him. I

mean he raked me over the coals and told me to toughen up
and keep this person happy. You know what makes this person
happy. Beating on the people around him. That is how he gets
his jollies. I watch him do it to his people. I have first hand
experience of him doing it to me. I hate going there. I would
love to take him to lunch and order his to go, BUT I can't."
    "Answer me a question. Does the company really make
a profit off his business?"
    "That's an interesting question. I have sat and
calculated the hours I spend with him, the amount of
concessions we make to him and the number of hours others
have to spend taking care of his problems and you know
what?"
    "I'll bet you lose money on him."
    "You are right. He is not a profit center. We lose
money on him. Not only that, he keeps people so upset they
are no good to the next person they have to deal with. Listen!
When I leave his place, I drive around for an hour dumping
what he has emotionally done to me. That hour costs the
company money."
    "Have you shared this financial stuff with your boss?"
    "You bet. I have sat with him and showed him in black
and white. Know what his response was? *He spends money
with us and that's all that matters.* How sick is that?"
    "Pretty sick. What does that say to you?"
    "It tells me I don't matter. It tells me I am just a thing
the company uses. It makes me feel like I have no presence
and no value."
    Recently, I received an email from George letting me
know he had left the company. His words were, "I finally had
all I could take. I tried one last time to approach my boss with
what this person was doing. He looked at me and called me a

weakling. I am not a weakling; I am someone who wants to do a good job, but if you cannot please someone, you need to move on. Richard, I don't fit in this environment."

Another quality person sacrificed because management couldn't face the fact *that the customer is not always right.* All management could see was dollar signs, not what the behavior of this negative customer was doing to the spirit of his people.

When you cannot please or satisfy a person, all you can do is appease them. Appeasing them validates their negative behavior and sends a negative message to all those who have to take care of them. The wear and tear these negative people bring to the environment does not make them an asset. The customer is not always right! When they are wrong, they should be told so. To validate their behavior is to devalue your internal customers. The result is an angry internal customer who loses respect for management and an empowered negative customer. Now, is that an environment where quality customer care can take place?

Customer Care Questions:
- *Is your company willing to fire negative customers?*
- *Does your company ask you to tolerate people who are only there to make waves?*
- *Do you believe that the customer is always right at any cost?*

What Behaviors Say You Should Fire The Customer?
F   fights with your people
I   insists on always being right
R   refuses to treat people with respect
E   emotional beatings

I Won't Help You!
If you aren't there to help the customer, you shouldn't be allowed to be there.

It was one of those travel days you know you are going to have, but pray you don't have. When it starts, you know it is just going to continue the entire travel day.

It started with the hotel forgetting to plug in my early morning wake up call. You know; you call down the night before and request they give you a wake up call at 3 A.M. Then, you lay in bed worrying whether you are going to wake up in time. Finally, around 1 A.M. you fall asleep. All of a sudden, you wake up, look at the clock and realize you didn't get your wake up call. You race around, make it downstairs, confront the front desk person to have them tell you, "We have been having a problem with the system. We don't know if people got their calls or not."

You race out the door, jump into a cab because you have missed the hotel shuttle, make a mad dash to the airport, check in and come face-to-face with the security line. On this particular day, those who are there to make sure your flight is safe didn't get their early morning coffee and are not in a good mood. I took my computer out of my bag, placed it in their little tray, took my money clip out of my pocket, put it in my briefcase, and explained to the person guiding things through that I had an LCD projector in my bag. He nodded and pushed it through.

I walked through the detector and was motioned over to a holding area. That was okay. They wand me and I walked over to pick up my things when I was grabbed by Attila the Hun. She barked at me "leave your things there and come over

If a customer service person is not there to help the customer, why are they there?

here with me." She motioned to another section and started to walk away.

I paused until she turned around and said, "I will be happy to come over there as soon as I gather my things."

She spun around, got this stern look on her face and barked, "You will leave them there and come with me."

I looked at her and said in a gentle, yet firm voice, "I will be happy to come over there as soon as I gather my things. I am not going to leave my computer and briefcase here."

She started back toward me and I knew this was going to be a battle. Just as she got close to me another security person stepped in-between us, looked at her and said, "It is okay for him to gather his things."

With that, I gathered my things and walked over to her. The look on her face told me I was in for it.

"Put your bags on this table and sit down in that chair."

Realizing there was no winning this battle, I placed my bags on the table and sat down. She then proceeded to take everything out of my briefcase and LCD bag. She then turned to me and barked in even a stronger voice than before, "Stand up and put your arms out."

She wanded me again and then told me I could go. I stood there and just looked at her. The look on her face was not a pleasant one.

I really do understand what they are doing and the reason they are doing it, but there has to be a better way of handling people. Flying is frightening enough for most people. Add to that fear a procedure that is filled with unhappy people who operate like robots and it is not a good situation.

I put my things back in my bags and made my way to the plane. I got on the plane to discover this lady, whose breathe told me she had had way more to drink than she should have, was sitting in my seat.

I walked back to the flight attendant, showed her my boarding pass and explained that someone was in my seat. She looked at me with a look that said, "I don't want to deal with this."

"Would you mind sitting in 1A?"

Now, normally taking another seat would not bother me, but 1A is the bulkhead and there is really no place for your luggage or your feet.

"If you don't mind, would you ask her to sit in 1A and I will take my assigned seat?"

Have you ever had someone give you a look that was evil in its intent? I got one from this flight attendant.

"I've already had one round with her. She is drunk and wanted a drink. I wouldn't serve her and she got upset with me."

I knew she was waiting for me to say, "Okay, just let her stay there." This was a three-hour flight and I didn't want to be stuck in the bulkhead after being on stage for four hours. I just stood there, and she got the message.

Making her way to the lady, she asked to see her boarding pass and explained she was in the wrong seat. In fact, her seat was 1A. The lady didn't want to move, but the flight attendant told her she would have to move.

Finally, I was in my seat and could relax. I was leaning back waiting for us to back away from the gate when the pilot came over the PA system.

"Ladies and gentlemen this is your Captain speaking. On behalf of myself, my First Officer and the rest of the crew I want to welcome you aboard our flight to Dallas/Fort Worth.

We are going to be detained here for a few more minutes. We have a warning light that tells us there is a problem we need to have checked. We have called maintenance and they are on their way. We don't anticipate it taking very long. As soon as I know something, I will get back to you. In the meantime, lean back and relax."

I was sitting in seat 3C and could see all that was happening. The look on the Captain's face told me we were going to be here for a while. That didn't really bother me. I had a two and a half hour layover in Dallas. I was going to have to sit somewhere and this was as good as any place.

The look on the Captain's face was correct. We just kept sitting there. Finally, whatever the situation was, was corrected and we were on our way.

Once airborne, the Captain came back on. "Folks, I am sorry for the delay. It is just one of those things that happens and we wanted to make sure the plane was safe. According to our computer, we should arrive in Dallas at 8:25 and be at the gate shortly there after."

I thought, "That will give me 35 minutes to make my connection. Maybe this day is going to take a turn for the better."

Traveling as much as I do, I knew that would be enough time. I leaned back and spent the flight doing some writing.

We arrived in Dallas right on the schedule the Captain had told us. We taxied to an area and came to a stop. Again, traveling as much as I do, I knew this was not the way to the terminal.

"Folks," the Captain announced. "I would like to welcome you to Dallas/Ft. Worth. That's the good news. It seems there is a plane at our gate and we are going to have to sit here for a few minutes. They tell me they are doing their final paper work and it shouldn't be long. I will keep you posted."

My mind told me, "This is not good. You are going to miss your connection."

We sat there for twenty minutes and finally made our way to our gate. One of the good things about traveling First Class is the ability to get off the plane in a hurry. We were parking at Gate 14 and my connection was leaving from Gate 36. Knowing it was going to be a hike, I put my walking mode into trot mode and away I went.

I arrived at the gate out of breath, but the jet way door was still open. That meant I had made it. I approached the counter, handed them my boarding pass and started toward the jet way.

The security person who was standing there said, "Would you mind stepping over here for random screening?"

I walked over and began the routine of having them go through my bags. I knew the routine, so I sat down and again took my shoes off and just waited. Finally, the random screening was over, and I made my way down the jet way to my seat. I entered the plane and started looking for a place for my LCD bag.

Now, if you travel, you know how much luggage people carry on. Since 9/11, they have limited it to two pieces, BUT the size of some of those pieces is unreal. With two pieces, you should put one piece under the seat and the other in the overhead bin. For some reason people feel, they need that space under their seat and they load the overhead with everything.

I opened every bin and there was no space to be found.

I knew there was space in the front coat closet, so I asked the Flight Attendant if I could put my bag there. I explained what was in the bag. He told me he would check with the lead Flight Attendant. He turned, went to the front of the plane and talked to the gentleman who was in charge. He turned, headed back to me and the look on his face told me he didn't have good news for me.

"He said you will have to put your bag in an overhead bin. I believe there is some room toward the back of the plane."

Now, I am in seat 3C and the back of the plane is row 36. The look on my face told him I wasn't happy with his answer.

"Is there no room in the front closet?"

"I think there is room. He just doesn't want your bag there."

"Can I talk to him?"

The startled look on his face told me that might not be a good idea. I knew there was no regulation against my bag being there, so I wanted to know why.

He turned, went back to the lead Flight Attendant, talked to him for a second and they both started toward me.

I looked at him and said, "I have checked all the overhead space here in first class and all the bins are full. Is there room for me to place my bag in the front closet?"

His look turned to one of defiance, he leaned in and with a very gruff voice he said, "I told the flight attendant you could not put your bag in there."

"Is there room?"

"It doesn't matter whether there is room; I said you could not put your bag there."

"Listen, I travel 200 days a year and I know there is nothing wrong with me putting my bag there. Why can't I put it there?"

His facial expression turned to anger as he responded with, "Because I said you can't. You can put it in the back of the plane or we can check it."

With that he stepped back and his facial expression said, "Go ahead; challenge me. There is no way I am going to help you."

The passenger across the aisle had been watching the exchange. He tapped my arm and said, "I'll put my bag under my seat and you can put your bag there." He got up, took his bag down and with that I placed my bag in the overhead.

After I stored my bag, I asked the Flight Attendant for his name. "My name is Lyle; what is your name?"

I told him my name and informed him I would be writing Delta a letter about his lack of customer care. He turned and walked away while muttering to himself.

The first Flight Attendant I talked to later came back to me and said, "I'm sorry for his behavior. He is not in a good mood and has been taking it out on people all day."

The gentleman who had removed his bag for me, looked at me and said, "And they wonder why people who travel for a living are upset today. His attitude has no place in a service position. If he was not having a good day, he should have either not been here or been put in the back galley where he didn't have to visit with the customer."

The challenge here is Lyle is not the exception; he is the rule in most service environments. The role of a service representative is more than a job; it is a responsibility. If those who have been given that responsibility of customer care are not there to take care of the customer, they should be removed. Their presence costs the company the respect and loyalty of the customer. I guess from the lack of action from management, customer respect and loyalty doesn't matter.

I think it can be summed up in the statement one person made to me. "If you don't like it, go somewhere else." I did!

He said in words what many say through their behavior. Today's customer hears what the behavior of the Lyle's of the world says and is no longer afraid to take their dollars and spend them somewhere else. When you are not there to help the customer, the customer will go somewhere else. I guess many companies feel *it is easier to find a new customer than it is to address their internal service issues.*

Customer Care Questions:
- *Is the behavior of the company representative important?*
- *Do you think the service sector of business has gotten better or worse?*
- *Would the behavior of Lyle be tolerated in the company where you work?*

What Tells The Customer You Are There To Help Them?
H   having patience and time to help
E   expressing concern for their needs
L   listening with ears and eyes
P   pleasant personality

MISSION CONTROL

The real mission of a company is not to get the customer in the door; it is to bring them back with a smile.

Okay, let's say it one more time. Customer service is a concept. Customer care is a demonstration. Customer satisfaction is a statement that says their experience was positive and they are willing to come back. Customer disappointment is a statement that says their experience was not positive and they are not willing to commit to doing more business with the company.

Reality is, every time the customer enters the door of a business they are going to exit either feeling customer satisfaction or customer disappointment. This door is not a physical door; it is the emotional connection point that is created each time the customer comes in contact with *any* aspect of the company. It is at this point the customer forms an opinion about the company and its people. It is at this point the customer determines whether the company cares more about them or their money. You see, a company doesn't get to define how good they are; the customers do that.

The company may have talked about customer service, but if the concept is not implemented through a program of customer care demonstrated through the behavior of their people, there is going to be confusion on the part of the customer.

The interesting part of all this *is customer satisfaction is such a simple thing to achieve.* All it takes is people who are employed to help the customer doing a quality job of customer care. It is about creating a business environment where the customer is respected and their business appreciated.

When the customer closes
the door behind them, they
won't be back and neither
will their money!

It is understanding what the customer represents; it is seeing the customer as an investment in building a better company through the behavior of the people today.

The real mission of any company should not be to get the customer through the door, but to make sure their experience is so positive they want to come back; that they want to do more business with that company. Without the customer spending their dollars, there is no company; without the company, there are no jobs.

Every company shares two things:
- *products/services*
- *people*

The products and/or services are what get the company noticed; the people who represent the company are what get the company remembered. Every time the customer comes in contact with any aspect of the company, they form an opinion about the company's commitment to customer care. Every time the customer comes in contact with any aspect of the company, they are going to make a decision about the business they are going to do with that company.

When the mission of the company is to get into their wallets, not bringing them back through the door, the company sets up a negative experience for the customer. The customer will remember that experience and use it as a decision-making fact in their business relationship with the company.

Hey, "Thank you; come again" means nothing to a disappointed customer. What are they thanking them for? Are they thanking them for the opportunity to disappoint them?

Why would a disappointed customer want to come back? If they were there to spend money by buying a product that would satisfy a need and ran into a person who wasn't there to help them, why would they want to come back? Do businesses really think the customer doesn't understand the power they have through their dollars? Many companies must feel the customer is stupid. Those companies treat their internal customers with disrespect, and those internal customers turn around and take their frustrations out on the external customers who are simply seeking to spend dollars to fulfill a need.

Think about this! What is so challenging about customer care? It really is a simple process of people taking care of people. It really is about creating an internal company environment that respects those who are part of the company's visual demonstration of customer care. It really is about the company seeing both the internal and external customer as a valuable part of growing their business.

I really do believe there are four things that destroy companies:

- *inconsistencies*
- *inefficiencies*
- *non-caring people*
- *tired management*

Inconsistencies are simply a contradiction that someone noticed. It is a company advertising how important their customers are and having the customer arrive and come face-to-face with a person who doesn't care.

Inconsistencies can be the lack of a consistent commitment to producing a quality product.

I had a conversation with the President of a Midwestern manufacturing company. He sat there, shook his head and talked to me with a look of disgust on his face.

"What we do here is not rocket science. We

manufacture a product we have manufactured for 32 years. We do the same job over and over, and we still do it wrong. Every time our product leaves this company, it creates our reputation with our customers. When we don't do it right, they are disappointed with us. When they are disappointed with us, it makes our competition look better. I have talked till I am blue in the face about the need to be consistent with our production and still it seems some of the people don't care. These inconsistencies are going to put us out of business."

Inconsistencies cost companies business. Inconsistencies frustrate the customer and make them question the business they do. When the customer goes away, so does the business.

The reality is *inconsistencies are the result of people who don't care.* They show up physically and go through a routine without caring about what they are doing.

Inefficiencies occur when you have to touch something more times than it should have been touched. These are the mistakes that just keep getting repeated.

A Regional Manager for a mid-sized sales company put it this way. "I don't get it. We seem to be mistake prone. We have given them the tools and the training. We have done everything except doing it for them, and we still end up having to redo what should have been done correctly the first time. Maybe we should do it for them."

"Doing it for them" would not improve the situation; it would only send a message that says *you don't have to be accountable.* One of the great mistakes companies make is they create environments that protect their non-committed people, rather than challenging them to step up or step away. As long as one is not held accountable and responsible for their behavior, there is no reason for them to care about improving.

Inefficiencies are simply a demonstration of a person who doesn't care how they do what they do. The result is a constant series of mistakes that someone has to clean up. Those mistakes punish the rest of the internal staff and frustrate the external customer who has to deal with them.

Non-committed people have become the rule, not the exception. Too many people work for a paycheck, not out of a sense of commitment and pride. Too many who go to work each day have quit before they get there, go through a routine and really don't care how they do what they do.

I know that sounds harsh, but look at the lack of quality coming from companies today. Look at the number of frustrated customers.

Know what? Corporate America would have been smarter never having started the customer service era. When they started talking about customer service, they raised the customer's expectations. That in turn created more customer connection points, which increased the possibility of the customer being disappointed.

The idea of customer service is a promise many chose not to live up to. It was a game to get the customer to feel like the company cared about them. The tragedy is it remains a concept because the company's people don't demonstrate the idea of customer care. That makes customer service a point of punishment for the customer, rather than an experience they enjoy.

The truth is *when people don't care; they demonstrate it through their behavior.* Remember, behavior never lies.

Put all this together and you get tired management. Many in management are exhausted. They are tired of pushing people to do what they are being paid to do. They are tired of going to work each day to fight fires they didn't create. They are tired of having upper leadership bark at them for the lack of productivity by the people. They are tired of fighting a battle they feel they can't win.

Ralph, a manager for a tire company in Arizona put it this way, "I used to think management would be fun. When I started with this company, I wanted to work my way up to being a branch manager. I must have been crazy. This job is not fun. It is exhausting; it is frustrating; it keeps me drained. I have just about had all I can take. I would rather go out and dig ditches, than deal with the crap I am handed on a daily basis. I have people who come here and hang out, not work. I have to constantly stay on their case to get them to perform. I have upper management calling and wanting to know why the numbers aren't what they want them to be. I try to talk to them about giving me the power to make decisions, but they don't want to hear that. They just want me to produce the numbers. I think I have finally realized I don't matter to them. I am simply an instrument to produce numbers, not a person who brings value. That hurts!"

Customer care is really very simple. It is about people caring about people. When that happens, there is going to be an environment where people inside have fun and translate that fun to those they do business with. That means the external customer is happy and does more business with the company, and the company is happy because they have the business from the customer. Tell me what is so difficult about this?

We both know the answer. It is the idea of people enjoying what they are doing because they work for a company that treats them as an asset, rather than a commodity to use to line their coffers.

When people feel they don't matter, they react with negative behaviors that weaken everything they touch. When people feel valuable and important, they respond with positive behaviors that strengthen their environments.

The result is an environment that either demonstrates customer care or creates customer disappointment. Is that so difficult to understand?

Customer Care Questions:
- *Do you feel you matter to your company?*
- *Could you do a better job of customer care?*
- *Are you in love with what you are doing? If not, why? If so, why?*

What Should The Real Mission Be?
M   making the customer feel important
I   investing in sharpening people skills
S   searching for ways to improve all that is done
S   staying focused on the customer
I   investigating where customer care isn't happening
O   owning up to mistakes
N   never taking the customer for granted

THE PEOPLE FACTOR
When people become a tool to be used, everyone loses.

I wasn't going to go see it, but I did. I thought it would be hokey, but it was actually pretty good. I am talking about the movie <u>Spiderman</u>. I had read a couple of the comic books and wasn't too impressed. I thought the movie would be just as corny, but one line in the movie made me glad I went.

There is a scene where Peter's aunt and uncle are having a conversation. They are talking about his being laid off from his job. In the middle of the conversation he makes this statement. "Companies are downsizing their people in order to upsize their profits."

What a powerful statement. The reality is *the statement is true.* Too many companies have stopped seeing their people as valuable. Too many companies have really stopped caring about the quality of customer care. Sure they preach customer service, but their behavior says something else.

Their behavior sends the message loud and clear. *We are more interested in our bottom-line than we are about our people and our customers.* All behavior has an agenda. All behavior makes a statement about true intentions. Companies can say what they want, but their behavior signals a very dangerous message that should make us sit up and pay attention. *The concept of Customer Service for many companies is a lie! All they really care about are the dollars they put in their bank accounts.*

Behavior never lies! When words say one thing, but behavior says another, that is a lie. If a company preaches customer service, but doesn't create an environment that is customer friendly, that is a lie.

Behavior Never Lies!

When companies no longer care about their people, their behavior is designed to punish them in order to fulfill their real agenda — *put money in their bank accounts no matter what the cost to humans.*

Isn't that what we learned from Enron? It is okay to lie; it is okay to steal; it is okay to use the trust of people to take advantage of them; it is okay to do whatever you want— just don't get caught. Who got punished in all this? Their top leadership didn't. The punishment was handed out to those who worked to deliver customer care. Many lost their entire life savings. Do you think the top leadership of Enron really cared? I haven't seen anything that says to me they did.

Isn't that the bottom line to the financial situation we find our nation struggling with today? Big corporations made decisions based on increasing their bottom line with very little thought about the consequences. Then, they cried about their financial situation and government bailed them out. Who got punished in all this? It's the people who believed that these companies cared. It's the people who put their trust in what they were told. The truth be known, those at the top of many of these companies had become cold and calculated. I believe all behavior has an agenda. For these "leaders" to say they didn't know what was happening was a lie. They just didn't care about what their behavior was doing. They didn't care about all the lives that would be affected.

They are not alone in their behavior. It has become standard practice within the halls of most companies. People have become a commodity, rather than an asset. The external customer has become a means to an end, rather than a treasure to protect. Customer Service has become a statement to deceive, rather than a fact that is demonstrated. Money has become the driving force; greed has become the agenda; people have become an object to use to fill their coffers; the bottom-line has become the only thing that matters.

The myth of customer service is constantly demonstrated by the behavior of those who live under the shroud of deception. To turn this around the top leadership of companies must get back to caring about those who are there to represent the company to their customers. The behavior of those on the front line is consistent with the message they are feeling from those above them. Let's stop blaming the front line people for their behavior. Let's start at the top and ask one question:

Are you more in love with your internal and external customers or your bottom-line?

The answer is apparent through their behavior. Leadership is the real issue and their people the demonstration of their presence. If we want to turn the quality of customer care around, start with the top. Maybe those who sit at the top and those who sit in their comfortable Boardroom chairs should come down and spend a day walking in the shoes of those who have to live with the decisions they make behind their closed doors. If those who have been given the responsibility of leading were really leaders, they would understand *profit is the result of quality people doing a quality job of customer care.*

If those who have accepted the role of being a leader were really leaders, they would make decisions based on what was best for their internal and external customers. They would make the treatment of people more important than putting more money in their pockets.

Maybe there is even more wisdom in the words of Peter's uncle than we realize. *They are downsizing people in order to upsize their profits.* The result of that has been the customer not believing in customer service, companies not being able to delivery quality customer care and a business environment that doesn't respect its internal or external customers. I think we have created a mess!

The real mission of any company should not be to get the customer through the door, but to create an experience so positive they want to come back.

Customer service is simply a concept defined by the people the external customer has to go through to do business with them. The reality is most companies preach the value of the customer, but don't deliver that message through the behavior of their people. The mission has become *take their money.* They don't value people; they value their dollars. They don't understand that profit is the result of quality people doing a quality job of customer care. Let's make taking care of the internal and external customer the mission!

Customer Care Questions:

- *Do you feel your company really cares about their people?*

- *Do you feel your company is really committed to improving the quality of their customer's experience?*

- *What do you think is the #1 area where your company needs to improve the quality of their customer's experience?*

Customer Care Is Really About:

C   making the customer feel important

A   investing in sharpening people skills

R   searching for ways to improve all that is done

E   staying focused on the customer

ONE LAST TIME

Customer Service – fact or fiction, concept or reality? That is the real concern!

I had a gentleman tell me one time, "Richard, it is easier to find new customers than it is to have to worry about taking care of the ones you have. They are not worth the effort!"

Where do you think his business is today? Everyday, in a multitude of ways, you are creating either customers for life or customers for a moment. The growth of business is learning the secret to creating *Customers For Life!* The key is creating a customer experience that separates you from all the others in a like business. To achieve this, what must you do?

Here is what I think the ultimate Customer Experience must be about:

- Caring for your customer is not an option; it is who you are.
- Understanding the Customer's need is a quest everyone is involved in discovering.
- Staying focused on them while they are there and after they leave.
- Taking the time with them to really allow them to feel you appreciate their business.
- Offering to commit the time to really understand their need.
- Making your company environment customer friendly.
- Expression of all your people is *we care about you and the business you bring to us.*
- Respecting them as a person and a customer is the statement our behavior will make.

When Customer Appreciation becomes the behavior that is demonstrated by all who represent your company, Customer Service will become a reality, not a concept. Now, you have your challenge! Make it happen.

ABOUT THE AUTHOR

Richard Flint is one of those unique people who has been given the ability to see the clarity in the midst of what looks confusing. Since 1980, he has been sharing his insights and philosophies with audiences all over North America. He is known as the person who knows you even though he has never met you. He has written 14 books, recorded over 50 audio albums/cds, and filmed 27 videos. Beyond being an author, he is a nationally recognized speaker, a lifestyle coach to many who are seeking to stop repeating and start achieving, and a frequent guest on radio and television talk shows. But more than all this, you will find him to be a friend whose understandings can calm your emotional confusion.

SERVICES AVAILABLE

On-site training, consulting and keynote speaking.
It's simple. Richard Flint can make your people better.
He can customize any of his programs and come right to your
company's door. He also provides a full range of in-house
consulting services, and is always delighted to add sparkle to
your next corporate or association meeting with a stimulating
keynote presentation designed just for you.

For more information about Richard's on-site services, call our
Marketing Department at 1-800-368-8255.

Whether you have 30 or 3,000 people to make better,
Richard Flint is the answer.

Share It With Others

To order copies of this book,
Call 1-800-368-8255
or (757) 873-7722
or visit
www.RichardFlint.com

Special quantity discounts are available
for bulk purchases.

Please allow 2-3 weeks for US delivery.
Canada & International orders
please allow 4-6 weeks for delivery.

<u>Other Books by Richard Flint, CSP:</u>

I Need A Life!

Behavior Never Lies

The Truth About Stress

Breaking Free

Building Blocks *For Strengthening Your Life*

Building Blocks *For Strengthening Your Relationships*

Building Blocks *For Improving Customer Relationships*

Building Blocks *For Controlling Stress*